DISCA

D0910453

AFTERWARDS
SLOVENIAN WRITING
1945-1995

SOUTH ORANGE PUBLIC LIBRARY

AFTERWARDS
SLOVENIAN WRITING
1945-1995

Edited by
Andrew Zawacki

SOUTH ORANGE PUBLIC LIBRARY

WHITE PINE PRESS · BUFFALO, NEW YORK

891.8
Aft

WHITE PINE PRESS
P.O. Box 236, Buffalo, New York 14201

Copyright ©1999 by White Pine Press

All rights reserved. This work, or portions thereof,
may not be reproduced in any form without permission.

This book contains works of fiction. Names, characters, places,
and incidents are either the product of the author's imagination
or are used fictitiously, and any resemblance to actual persons,
living or dead, events, or locales is entirely coincidental.

Publication of this book was made possible, in part,
by grants from the New York State Council on the Arts
and the Slovenian Ministry of Culture.

Acknowledgments: Portions of this anthology were originally printed in an earlier version distributed solely in Europe as The Imagination of Terra Incognita: Slovenian Writing 1945-1995, edited by Aleš Debeljak
(Fredonia, NY: White Pine Press, 1997).

Grateful acknowledgments are made to the editors, authors, translators, agents, heirs, and publishers of the
following publications, for permission to reprint the material in this anthology:

Excerpts from Pilgrim Among the Shadows by Boris Pahor, English translation by Michael E. Biggins, copyright ©1995 by Harcourt Brace & Company, reprinted by permission of the publisher.
Acknowledgments continue on page 242.

"Large Letter, 1964" by Janez Bernik (oil/ canvas, 140 x 200 cm) is reprinted
on the cover by permission of the Museum of Modern Art, Ljubljana.

Book design: Elaine LaMattina

Printed and bound in the United States of America

1 3 5 7 9 10 8 6 4 2

Library of Congress Cataloging-in-Publication Data

Afterwards : Slovenian writing, 1945-1995 / edited by Andrew Zawacki.
p. cm. — (Terra Incognita ; 4)
ISBN 1-877727-97-0 (alk. paper)
I. Zawacki, Andrew, 1972-   . II. Series : Terra incognita
PG1961.E1A37   1999
891.8'408005—dc21   99-43487
CIP

For Tina Verovnik
and for
Dušan Šarotar

eni tečejo vodoravno, drugi stojijo navpično,
z rokami se jih domače oprijemljemo

1341 6130180 11.00

CONTENTS

FICTION

Introduction

Andrew Zawacki

"On my desk is a piece of barbed wire from the Austria-Hungary border. That was the whole point, after all, wasn't it? To have pieces of wire on our desks, not running through our fields."
— *Drago Jančar*

The First Balkan War began in 1912 and ended just in time for a second to take its place the following year. While Slovenia was not engaged in these wars involving nearby nations, all the selections in this volume implicitly bear the cicatrice of those imperialist conflicts, which in some measure initiated the breakup of the Austro-Hungarian Empire and the formation of the Kingdom of Serbs, Croats and Slovenes. Each selection follows the ensuing war to end all wars and, because it didn't, the Second World War. These essays, poems and short fiction come after the rise of Marshal Tito and the social revolution of 1941-1945, as well as the break from Stalin three years later that enabled a "Yugoslav road to socialism." Some of the selections postdate Tito's death in 1980 and the subsequent collapse of Communism in the Republic of Yugoslavia. A few were written around the Ten Day War between Slovenia and the Serb-led Yugoslav Army in 1991, when Slovenia declared its independence. This book is thus published when Slovenian statehood, which persisted early on despite a Third Balkan War fought just across its eastern borders, is only eight years old. The complex roots of this country of Southern Slavs, however, extend back for centuries, through a rich but not always nurturing heritage. That inheritance is interrogated and variously affirmed or disputed by a number of the writers in these pages, with the informed urgency generally associated with current events.

While no one writing in Slovenia would pretend to ignore the historical context of its literary tradition, the writers featured here have nonetheless refused to allow seemingly endless military and political insecurities to debilitate a long and longing view of personal drama. It is doubtful, when compiling an anthology of Slovenian writing of the latter half of this century, that "there could be," in the words of American poet Robert Duncan, "a book without nations in its chapters." Yet the confused, confusing questions of Europe, ethnicity, empire and autonomy are often only backdrop to what many of these writers have sought to foreground, namely, an attention to private life and its attendant sorrows and joy. The news tells us that ideologues of the sort that perpetrated a so-called final solution are still trying to run the show in the former Yugoslavia in this last decade of the millennium, and are too often succeeding as the West and the rest of the world entertain ideas of doing something about it. Contemporary Slovenian writers are all too aware of Sarajevo, Srebrenica, Vukovar, Omarska, Kosovo—in short, of what Croatian journalist Branka Magaš has called "the old recipe" of "kill one-third, expel one-third, and assimilate one-third," a recipe, one hardly need add, severely less generous in recent years. Indeed, Slovenian literati have been among the most outspoken advocates of freedom and justice not only within their own country but also on behalf of their neighbors. Yet in their work Slovenian authors still insist upon fidelity to a personal, if not interpersonal dialogue that, far from belying these tragedies, in fact redeems them. Remembering thousands awaiting the grave, Bosnian poet Izet Sarajlić addressed another, "Oh my little one / My great love / Tonight let's love each / Other in their name." Such a poignant, reverent plea for intimacy amid destruction may be the hallmark of the most engaging writing in Central Europe, from which Slovenia is emerging as a crucial, distinctive voice.

One limitation of that voice is the discouraging lack of writing by Slovenian women promoted in Slovenia. It is difficult to account for why so apparently little is endorsed by official channels within the country, but it may be that the socio-political situation in the former Yugoslavia did not encourage writing by women or foster its publication. A significant group of Croatian female writers, however, has managed to surface as a distinct movement of *"écriture feminine,"* their books translated into English and often into French. Despite the growing notoriety within Slovenia of, say, fiction writer Maja Novak and poets Maja Vidmar and Taja Kramberger, it is not clear why contemporary female Slovenian writers have been denied the international visibility accorded to their Croatian counterparts. Given the success of Slovenian novelist Brina Švigelj in France, where she's lived for two decades, one wonders if Slovenian female writers don't have to live abroad to be read abroad. I would urge readers interested in tracing the negligence toward female Slovenian authors to consult Zdravko Duša's essay in *The Veiled Landscape*, the first and only English-language anthology of Slovenian women's writing, published by the Slovenian Office for Women's

Policy in 1995. Most relevantly, Duša argues that contemporary Slovenian literature does not have a female author who would signify some "trademark of national women's writing" to readerships outside Slovenia. In any event, the major publishing houses and literary institutes have traditionally been directed by men, with a few exceptions such as Mira Mihelič, a former president of the Slovene P.E.N., and university appointments have by and large been occupied by males as well. Everything indicates this is changing for the better, though it does not necessarily make a responsible, curious editor's task easier in the present. On the other hand, I am aware that I may be equally responsible for this volume's gender imbalance, on the grounds suggested by Australian poet and editor Tracy Ryan when she asks, "Is it possible that many editors do not 'see' a good woman-authored poem because their template automatically excludes it?"

Another limit to the reception of Slovenian literature on this side of the Atlantic is linguistic. While the majority of Slovenian authors are quite capable if not sophisticated, avid readers of literature written in English, there are few American writers who can read Slovenian literature in the original. For starters, the Slovenian language is only spoken by two million people, to say nothing of many Americans' disinterest in learning any language other than their own. The fact remains that it is extremely difficult to find English translations of Slovenian literature, let alone translations of high quality. There are, thankfully, several extremely competent and felicitous translators of Slovenian into English, both in and outside the U.S. and Slovenia, most of whom are responsible for the translations comprising this book. American and Slovenian writers and readers, though, can only benefit from an increasing interest in the exchange of literature between their respective countries, and I sincerely hope that more scholars, poets, fiction writers and professional translators will engage in rendering Slovenian literature into English.

American literature has contributed significantly to the formation of Slovenian letters over the past fifteen years, in part because Slovenian writers have been keen to fill the space that opened in Communism's wake with less politically antagonistic stanzas and chapters. In turn, Slovenian writing, in particular Slovenian poetry, has begun to make its presence felt among a generation of younger American writers eager for a strenuous, often fabular subject matter and a more finely tuned subversive sensibility. The poetry of Edvard Kocbek, Slovenia's most internationally recognized poet since the Second World War, has been well-received in the U.S. for decades. Tomaž

Šalamun's poems have found a welcome audience among American poets and critics since the late 1960s, and his work is currently being newly championed by the generation of American poets born during that era. Since the early 90s, Aleš Debeljak has carved a unique place for himself in U.S. literary and academic circles as a poet and cultural critic. Among fiction writers, Drago Jančar has been Slovenia's most consistent bid for the Nobel Prize and, along with Andrej Blatnik, has been widely translated and frequently published in the U.S.. That is not to say that numerous other Slovenian writers have not made their way into books and journals published here. Kajetan Kovič, Veno Taufer, Dane Zajc and Gregor Strniša, for instance, were all included in Vasa D. Mihailovich's *Contemporary Yugoslav Poetry*, published by the University of Iowa Press in 1977, to name only one major introduction of Slovenian poetry to an American audience. A younger generation of Slovenian poets, especially Jure Potokar, Alojz Ihan, Brane Mozetič, Uroš Zupan and Aleš Šteger, is gaining justifiably greater recognition in the States.

English-speaking readers, if persistent, have enjoyed a substantial number of small-press books by Slovenian authors and anthologies devoted solely to Slovenian literature, which a glance at the acknowledgments to this volume will demonstrate. Until now, however, there has not been available within the United States a volume collecting post-War Slovenian poetry, fiction, essays and memoirs. While this book attempts to cover as much historical and aesthetic ground as possible, it does not claim to be in any sense comprehensive. The sheer amount of Slovenian writing since 1945 and the relative unanimity regarding its dissemination and critical reception within and beyond Slovenia preclude such a claim. In some cases I have included what simply could not be overlooked, for reasons of historical or literary significance. In other cases I have included what I believe American readers might find interesting or provocative. I hope that in most cases these dual considerations of representation and delight are one and the same. It goes without saying that I have had to leave out many texts, if not a few deserving authors as well, which I admire or feel others might admire, usually in the interest of privileging what "works best" in translation. Among those writers regrettably omitted are Louis Adamic, Evald Flisar, Herbert Grün, Andrej Hieng, Lojze Kovačič, Florjan Lipuš, Neža Maurer, Mira Mihelič, Iztok Osojnik, Marjan Rožanc, Rudi Šeligo, Ifigenija Zagoričnik Simonovič, Ivo Svetina and Saša Vegri, not to mention an entire set of dramatists, foremost being Dominik Smole. One notable exclusion is the philosopher Slavoj

Žižek, whose work, even if it does not fall outside the parameters of a "literary" publication such as this, has already achieved the utmost prominence not merely in the U.S. but throughout Europe and farther afield. So while this anthology is designed to apprise American readers of much Slovenian literature written over the past half-century, it begs to be followed by other volumes, each preferably revising the previous, even if that should mean continuing to reprint some texts deemed indispensable.

The title of this anthology is intended to emphasize that what came before the words in its pages is integral to understanding those words. Yet the most exhilarating aspect of post-1945 Slovenian literature is its relentless ability to honor whatever dénouement has preceded its aspirations, while turning repeated exhaustions into an occasion for new song. Coming as they do after Auschwitz, after art, and after so many grand narratives that the end of the twentieth century is apparently ushering out—among them history itself—these writings testify not only to what has been lost but also, more importantly, to what remains and what may lie ahead.

Ithaca, New York
August 1999

Essays

Slovenia: A Brief Literary History

Aleš Debeljak

What is Slovenia? Where is Slovenia? These were the questions most commonly raised in July 1991 when Slovenia, one of the six constituent republics of Yugoslavia, briefly made the headlines all over the Western world. That long hot summer saw the first open military conflict on European soil since the end of the Second World War. The ten-day war between the national militia and the Yugoslav army, and its larger consequences, brought about major changes on the European political map. Riding on the heels of the collapse of the Soviet empire in 1989, the end of the communist *ancien régime*, and German unification, Slovenia's nation-wide public plebiscite, democratic elections and declaration of independence formed the legal foundation for its successful defense against the communist-led Yugoslav army. For the first time in the long history of this tenacious Alpine Slavic people, Slovenians were free to live in an independent state of their own, fully responsible for their own collective existence. This paramount event had been vaguely prefigured, romantically hoped for, and, against all rational odds, anticipated by many Slovenian writers and poets.

Writers were traditionally invested with the uneasy obligation and the concomitant risk of acting as the keepers of the national flame, guardians of the moral, social and spiritual values embedded in the Slovenian culture and its language. It was precisely the language that represented the foremost national treasure and was a distinctive mark of identity for the Slovenian people, since historically they lacked many other full-fledged political, economic, or social institutions that might have helped shoulder the burden of maintaining and deepening a sense of national commitment.

It thus makes perfect sense to look for an answer to the questions, "What is Slovenia? Where is Slovenia?" in the meandering history of Slovenian letters. Indeed, one is invited to wonder what the writers and poets are like in this country that was until recently seen as the *terra incognita* of Central Europe, a country where more than two thousand books are published each year for the tiny population of two million, and where poetry books are routinely printed in editions of five hundred to three thousand copies.

Books on Central Europe describe Slovenia as a small patch of land squeezed between the snow-covered Alps and the warm Adriatic Sea. Forests cover more than fifty percent of Slovenia, a land sprinkled with hills, the tops of which are seldom without a typical baroque church—an indelible signature of Central European culture. Slovenia's capital, Ljubljana, emerged on the site of the ancient Roman garrison-camp, Emona, halfway between Vienna and Trieste. These towns were connected by the "southern railway," the lifeline of commercial and cultural life in the former Austro-Hungarian Empire. In the southern Slovenian lands, charming olive plantations nestle on the Mediterranean coast, while to the northeast the country sprawls into the vast Hungarian plains. To the north, the Karavanke mountain range separates it from Austria and from the large Slovenian ethnic minority in Carinthia, Austria's southernmost region.

While most Slovenians live in the Republic of Slovenia, considerable ethnic minorities continue to exist in Italy, Hungary, and Austria. In the nineteenth and twentieth centuries, numerous emigrants carrying Italian, Austro-Hungarian, and, later, Yugoslavian passports arrived on the shores of America. Like many other immigrants, Slovenians had fled from exploitation and foreign domination. Yet unlike many other emigrant groups, Slovenians left behind an emotional home, not a political state of their own. Their suitcases were loaded with books that, instead of contemplating a heroic military tradition and deeds of the sword, were permeated with deeds of the pen. The foundation of their national identity was kept alive in melancholic elegies, lyrical poems of sorrow and grief.

Culture, literature, and language were the pillars of the fragile identity of this nation, both at home and in exile. After the Second World War, the tragic wave of anti-Communist "displaced persons" in Argentina's immigrant community could not make do without books in their mother tongue. Since the Communist blockade prevented them from receiving books from their native country, they themselves wrote, translated, and published an impressive number of works. For Slovenians, even in times of struggle for bare existence, books were as vital for survival as loaves of bread.

Poets and writers were not only priests of language, but also politicians in disguise. In the absence of social, political, economic, and cultural institutions, poets and writers took on the role of guardians of the mother tongue and individualism, moral independence, and national integrity. The history of Slovenia is not a history of great military victories but a history of tenacious literary and linguistic guerrilla resistance to foreign rule. For all practical purposes, Slovenian history is a history of the Slovenian language, a language which in addition to singular and plural, also uses a dual form—one of the very few world languages that boast of such a rarity—which makes it extraordinarily suitable for intimate, personal, and erotic confessions.

But the Slovenian language was forced to assume a more pragmatic role: it had to give voice to ethnic and national sentiments. Due to centuries-long domination by foreigners, these sentiments were more a gentle whisper than an angry shout. National identity, however, remained at the core of the popular imagination, buoyed by an unrelenting belief that the expression of one's national and ethnic identity is a self-evident right. Today, these rights are taken for granted; unfortunately, the history of Slovenia profusely demonstrates that there were precious few rights that Slovenians could take for granted.

NATIONAL HISTORY, LITERARY HISTORY

Even with a hundred years of independence and sovereignty, the state of Carantania—King Samo's country of Slavs in the seventh century—could not be sustained. However, traces of Carantania have survived in more than the mighty stone throne now kept in an Austrian museum. The spirit of the first state of Slovenia and its democratic procedures is very much present in important historical records.

The ancient ritual for the installation of Carantanian dukes, carried out in the Slovenian language, whereby the Slovenian peasants transferred sovereign power to make laws for the community to the dukes, fascinated the celebrated humanist Aeneas Silvius Picolomini, later known as Pope Pius II. Following his extensive travels through Slovenian lands, he complimented this political ritual in his book, *Cosmographia Pii Papae De Europa* (1509), calling it "second to none." The French legal historian and philosopher Jean

Bodin, encouraged by Picolomini's tireless praise, examined the ritual in detail and described it as an original idea for transference of sovereignty that "had no parallel throughout the world." His book *Les Six Livres de la Republique* (1576), in which he wrote this generous praise, remains a classical reference for contractual political theory and is said to have inspired Thomas Jefferson when he wrote the draft of his Declaration of Independence.

Yet, even such democratic rules did not help Slovenians sustain their independence after King Samo's death. Franks, Bavarians, Charlemagne, Hungarians, Teutons, and later the Austro-Hungarian Empire became enemies whose belligerent armies advanced toward the warm waters of the Adriatic Sea, setting up political and economic institutions, fighting for money, lands and souls in the heart of Slovenian country. It is thus a real wonder that Slovenians managed to preserve their identity. In the absence of a nation-state of their own, the only real home for Slovenians was carved out in their language and creative imagination.

WRITERS AS SPOKESMEN OF THE PEOPLE

Although written records in Slovenian (sermons, confessions, poems) sporadically appeared from the eighth century on, it was the half century of the Reformation that gave Slovenians a systematic orthography, alphabet, and standardized language. The first book in Slovenian appeared in 1550, and a few years later Slovenians could read the Old and New Testaments in their mother tongue. Slovenian literature was given birth by Protestant preacher and writer Primož Trubar. On the wings of the Reformation movement, Trubar published his twenty-two books in Germany after having fled the religious persecution of the Catholic counter-Reformation in his native Slovenia. From Germany he smuggled books to Ljubljana to be clandestinely distributed across Slovenian lands.

Slovenians immediately recognized writers as the true and only political authorities. Their artistic work was invested with a single aim: to raise national consciousness. This was anything but easy. Theirs was a small nation where the middle class communicated in Italian and German; Slovenian was reserved for the lower classes, "for peasants and horses," as it was ironically put by Edvard Kocbek in his wonderful poem, "The Lippizaners."

Once Roman Catholicism became the dominant religion in the Habsburg Empire to which Slovenia belonged, education was given over to the Jesuits.

They utilized generous financial support from Archduke Ferdinand and established a college in Ljubljana as early as 1595. This provided the foundation for higher education in the Slovenian lands. The best and brightest Slovenians, however, continued to pursue their advanced studies in traditional Central European centers of learning: Prague or Cracow or, for the most part, cosmopolitan Vienna.

Later came the short-lived, albeit productive, French rule. The four years of Napoleonic regime were ushered in with the establishment of the Ilyrian Provinces (1809-1813) extending along the Adriatic coast all the way to Dubrovnik. For the first time, two-thirds of the ethnic Slovenian territory was brought together under one administrative and legislative command. The French labored hard to institute the Slovenian language in elementary schools, consequently promoting it as the everyday language of the middle class. Napoleon's regime emphasized the meaning of local languages to an extent inconceivable to the Habsburgs. Slovenian intellectuals and writers thus conveniently familiarized themselves with the French *esprit du temps* which was pregnant with nationalism. The ideas of the French Enlightenment were accepted by Slovenians as soon as they appeared while their political, economic, and organizational implementation in the 'Ilyrian Provinces' and its capital, Ljubljana, was immediate.

The first accomplished Slovenian poet, Valentin Vodnik (1758-1819), although a Roman Catholic priest, did not write exclusively for religious purposes, but was also devoted to the secrets of everyday life. It was certainly no accident that he developed his voice under the influences of the Enlightenment.

Predictably, Slovenian national self-consciousness reached its peak in Romanticism and in this respect did not lag behind the other Central European peoples that emerged out of "the Spring of Nations." However, the relentless pressure of German culture and continuous political subjugation from the House of Habsburg made it difficult to envision Slovenian survival. The common prediction had it that the Slovenians would pass into oblivion as a distinct ethnic community.

Slovenians, however, proved these speculations wrong. As early as the mid-nineteenth century, Slovenian literary magazines and journals began to be published in Ljubljana that cautiously, yet with increasing perseverance, tried to come to terms with national and political identity. Having been traditionally denied one, Slovenian writers put national identity at the core of their work.

A Toast To Freedom

The work of France Prešeren (1800-1849), the most revered Slovenian poet, best encapsulates the national longing for freedom and independence. By profession a free-minded lawyer and by vocation a Romantic poet, Prešeren wrote in German, the Central European *lingua franca*, as fluently as in Slovenian. Yet for him there was no dilemma: Slovenian was not merely his mother tongue, but the language of choice and an article of political faith. In the Slovenian language, he created in the best Orphean tradition works known by every Slovenian. A genuine Romantic poet of great creative power accompanied by a great capacity for alcohol, Prešeren's private life was suffused with disillusion. His ethereal Laura was a daughter from a respectable bourgeois house, and in spite of all the beautiful and passionate poems he dedicated to her, she married a German nobleman. But what Prešeren did not achieve in his private life he did accomplish on a national level: he succeeded in uniting all Slovenians in one spiritual community.

Prešeren's poem "A Toast to Freedom" is today the national anthem. Back in 1848, however, the censors of Chancellor Metternich's regime in Vienna correctly identified the revolutionary potential in the lyrical metaphors whereby Prešeren called for the union of all Slovenians, if necessary by military resistance to domination:

> To whom with acclamation
> And song shall we our first toast give?
> God save our land and nation
> And all Slovenians where'er they live,
> Who own the same
> Blood and name,
> And who one glorious Mother claim.
>
> Let thunder out of heaven
> Strike down and smite our wanton foe!
> Now, as it once had thriven,
> May our dear realm in freedom grow.
> May fall the last
> Chains of the past
> Which bind us still and hold us fast!

Prešeren not only achieved symbolic unification, but also radically redefined Slovenian metaphors, established aesthetic standards, and dramatically expanded the limits of linguistic expression. Each and every person could recognize herself in the poetic description of the universal human condition. The poet's message about freedom and peace was not nationally exclusive. It rang true for all people:

> God's blessing on all nations
> Who long and work for that bright day,
> When o'er earth's habitations
> No war, no strife shall hold its sway;
> Who long to see
> That all men free
> No more shall foes,
> But neighbors be.

("A Toast to Freedom," translated by Janko Lavrin)

Prešeren's poetry accomplished something of a miracle. With the poems in which national and individual destiny blend into one universal message about liberation, Prešeren managed to rekindle the subdued flame of national self-consciousness. He turned language from a means of expression into the metaphysical foundation of national substance and the manifestation of national identity.

PURSUIT OF INDEPENDENCE

Ivan Cankar (1876-1918), the most important Slovenian fiction writer, was a legitimate counterpart to Prešeren in light of the impact his ideas and metaphors had on the nation. Having studied and lived in Vienna for a decade, Cankar was consistently addressing the role of artist as an outsider and the tensions between the provincial home and the cosmopolitan polis. However, when Cankar returned in 1910 from Vienna to Ljubljana he did so to be "in the center of life." This focus on national substance coupled with European form stood at the core of the far-reaching aesthetic program of "Slovenska moderna" (1895-1914), the first modern Slovenian artistic movement, to which Cankar made considerable contributions.

Cankar, described by Italian poet Eugenio Montale as a giant of European literature, was the first Slovenian writer to make a living from writing alone. His wealth of short stories, novels, plays, and essays critically undermined many Slovenian myths while creating new ones. Cankar's fictional depiction of the mother figure, for example, who sacrifices herself to support her son and thus envelopes him in a dialectic of guilt and affection, has become part of the collective self-understanding of Slovenians. Cankar worked his way through numerous aesthetic styles at the *fin-de-siècle*, refusing to align himself with any for too long. A revered bohemian and a challenging writer, Cankar must be credited with having introduced full-fledged modernism into Slovenian literature.

Cankar's astute political commentaries made it clear that the new Southern Slavic union, which he called for as early as 1913, should provide only a common political frame. The peoples and cultural traditions entering this new entity, Cankar claimed, were too diverse for "an illusionary, homogenous nation-state." His ideas maintained a forceful hold on the Slovenian imagination in every crisis during the development of the Yugoslav experiment, including the Slovenian summer of 1991 and subsequent independence.

Just as Cankar predicted, the disintegration of the Austro-Hungarian Empire in the wake of the First World War compelled Slovenians to seek greater freedom in a new common state of the Southern Slavs called the Kingdom of Serbs, Croats, and Slovenians, later renamed Yugoslavia. At first glance, the new union appeared to offer an ideal solution to the small Slovenian nation.

In 1919 the Slovenian language became the language of instruction at the newly established University of Ljubljana. Slovenians could finally use their national idiom without restrictions. Accordingly, they committed themselves to cultural life with extraordinary vigor, enthusiasm, and creative drive.

Slovenian writer Louis Adamic (1898–1951), who emigrated to the United States in his boyhood and later became, in the tradition of Upton Sinclair, a prominent American writer on social issues, produced a number of realistic novels and short stories in his adopted language, English. In one of his books Adamic described his home country during a visit he made before the Second World War as a Guggenheim fellow:

> Gradually I realized what I had dimly known in my boyhood that, next to agriculture, Slovenia's leading industry was Culture. In Lublyana were seven large bookshops (as large as most of the hardware, dry goods, and drugstores in town), two of them more than a hundred years old... Besides, each bookstore carried a

selection of the latest German, French, Czech, Serbo-Croat, English and Italian books... In Slovenia nearly everybody—merchants, peasants, priests, teachers, students—bought books anyhow... In two years there had been forty-eight performances of Hamlet in Lublyana. Most of the city's streets are named after poets, essayists, novelists, dramatists, grammarians. The largest monument in town is to the poet France Prešeren... When students take hikes into the country, their destinations usually are the graves and birthplaces of poets, dramatists, and other writers.

(The Native's Return, 1934)

Adamic's perspective was correct but incomplete. The situation was emphatically not as idyllic as it appeared to the sentimental visitor keen to see only flattering aspects of life in the land of his youth.

Due to changes in borders after the First World War, a significant number of Slovenians found themselves living in Italy. One third of Slovenians had to become, like it or not, Italian citizens, and their Slovenian descent made them second-rate citizens in Mussolini's state. Slovenians came under strong Fascist pressure: their press was prohibited, their schools were closed, priests could only hold illegal masses in clandestine locations. Many emigrated, but many more continued their struggle for national and cultural freedom, for the freedom to speak their mother tongue.

The importance of the Mediterranean to Slovenian life is demonstrated by the fact that it was not in landlocked Ljubljana but in Trieste—a cosmopolitan Adriatic port which, in 1918, was one of the three cities with the largest Slovenian population, the others being Ljubljana and Cleveland, Ohio—that some Slovenian intellectuals planned to establish their university. It would not have lasted long. Public use of the Slovenian language subjected those who dared to challenge the Fascist-imposed hegemony of Italian to high fines and imprisonment. Teachers of Slovenian were exiled; right-wing squads burned to the ground the Slovenian National House, the principal Slovenian cultural institution in the heart of Trieste. The Fascist battle cry *eia eia alala* eerily echoed throughout Slovenian neighborhoods, and Slovenian nationalists were murdered. Trieste made a pleasant retreat for James Joyce, an English teacher at the Berlitz language school there, but for Slovenians the city was a linguistic and cultural straight-jacket. While Italians and Austrians were charmed by Trieste's numerous promenades and well-mannered aristocratic circles, the Slovenian collective experience speaks of an oppressive place, a true "heart of darkness."

Boris Pahor (b.1913), an indefatigable advocate of the Slovenian minority's rights in Italy and a prolific fiction writer from Trieste, provides a fleeting glimpse of this uneasy ethnic cohabitation, though it is cloaked in his literary witness of months spent in a Nazi concentration camp, in his wonderfully moving memoir, *Pilgrim Among the Shadows* (1967).

In the southern Austrian region of Carinthia, the site of the first independent Slovenian state, the notorious brown shirts, Nazi thugs, terrorized Slovenians, vandalized their homes, and beat students and peasants. The former capital of the empire, Vienna, was in geographical terms little more than three hundred miles away; in terms of the human and national rights of the Slovenian minority, it could have been on another planet.

Writing in the mother tongue was an act of political and existential commitment for any member of the Slovenian ethnic minority in Austria, and it wasn't until well after the end of the Second World War that the situation changed. With the work of Florjan Lipuš (b.1937) this body of Slovenian literature most convincingly adopted a necessary form of aesthetic autonomy. Lipuš's refreshingly modernist credo made it possible for him to disregard national consciousness-raising as part of the literary endeavor. Instead, he delved into the depths of Slovenian language and its Carinthian dialects that have almost hermetically retained some of the most archaic words and idioms.

Outside Austria the situation between the world wars was admittedly better than in Italy, though hardly encouraging. Slovenian hopes were squarely invested in the formation of a political union with their "brethren" South Slavs. The Yugoslav union was believed to provide solid political and economic protection and, at the same time, to enable Slovenians to commence a fully-developed national life. Some foundations for such life had been laid out in the form of the first Slovenian university, the academy of arts and sciences, the national library, the theater and opera houses with Slovenian as an official language, and with the entirely Slovenian school system that had replaced both the bilingual German-Slovenian and the entirely German educational model of the pre-Yugoslav era.

Despite these advancements in national life, Slovenian aspirations for full autonomy soon collapsed. Serbian, the language of the royal court and of the most populous nation in Yugoslavia, became the language of public and official communication. High officials of the centralized state institutions came from Belgrade, more than five hundred miles from Ljubljana. Slovenian intellectuals were routinely appointed to posts in the heart of Bosnia, Serbia, and Montenegro. Slovenian became a second-rate language in the common South Slavic state. Later the regime in Belgrade, which since 1929 had been a dictatorship, tried to eradicate Slovenian identity on a nominal level, as well. It arranged for Slovenia to comprise, with selected western Croatian districts, an administrative province without a distinct national name.

But Slovenian persistence did not relax. Vibrant literary life reflected the aesthetic trends of Paris and Vienna. Newspapers and magazines, student clubs and, most notably, coffee houses provided public forums for young people to recite their rebellious poems and give heated lectures. Among the *literati*, the most radical was the prodigal son of avant-garde writing Srečko Kosovel (1904-1926), of whom Claudio Magris, an Italian expert on Central European letters, admiringly said in his book *Trieste: An Identity of the Border* (1987), "In Kosovel's lyrical poems a certain landscape and a human condition—the Karst and the Slovenian exclusion—reach a universal dimension for they turn into symbols of general situation and of a certain time in European civilization." Kosovel's equal, though more socially reticent, was the psychoanalytic playwright Slavko Grum (1901-1949), whose play *An Event in the City of Goga* for many decades provided a metaphor for the suffocating conditions the avant-garde writers wanted to transcend. Literary debates on expressionism, constructivism and surrealism were imbued with political overtones. This uneasy bond between politics and literature became a question of life and death after the Nazi invasion of Yugoslavia in 1941.

Prešeren's poetic ideal, "Better to die than to be a slave," once again provided moral, existential and national guidance. Most, though not all, writers joined the partisans and fled to the woods where, in the midst of the raging war, they printed their books, newspapers and magazines in makeshift print shops. In temporarily-liberated areas they organized literary readings, published reviews, and vigorously encouraged people to resist occupation. Needless to say, many of them died for freedom while writing and fighting.

Ljubljana is perhaps the only European capital where a visitor will look in vain for monuments to generals and victorious cavalrymen. Despite the liberation war and the revolution, Slovenians continue to be more attracted by the pen than the sword. Instead of generals, Slovenians placed poets on their pedestals of privilege. As noted by Louis Adamic, many streets are named after celebrated masters of the pen, and their faces solemnly gaze from the banknotes of independent Slovenia. During the Second World War, many Slovenian partisan brigades were named after poets and writers, another historically rare example of the vital importance of literature to this nation.

After the war many writers entered government office. A renowned pre-war poet, partisan and Christian Socialist, Edvard Kocbek (1904–1981), became vice-president of the Slovenian government and a minister in the federal Yugoslav government. He remained there until he fell out of favor for his refusal to give up his literary mission. Kocbek's poems, stories, and voluminous journals bear witness to his courage to criticize the black-and-white communist aesthetics of his former colleagues.

Kocbek's was the poetic pursuit of truth and the fight for freedom that guards language against authoritarian "newspeak." Educated both in Slovenia and in France, Kocbek was also the first to muster enough courage to expose to the public the most fiercely guarded communist secret: the liberation war was, to a considerable degree, a civil war between the "reds"and the "whites." The Liberation Front, a coalition of resistance groups established in 1941, was committed to fighting against the occupying forces. Communists, as one of the parties in the coalition, orchestrated an underground coup d'etat in 1943 and began running the resistance movement according to their political agenda, i.e., the social revolution. Simultaneous with the war of liberation, a tragic fratricidal war of communist-led partisans, "reds," against Slovenian Nazi-and-Fascist-collaborators, "whites," took place, primarily in and around Ljubljana.

After the war, collaborationist forces and their supporters retreated to the Allied-controlled territory of southern Austria. The Allies returned them to Tito's partisans who, in turn, killed as many as nine thousand to twelve thousand people. Against the imperative of complicity and silence, Kocbek publicly denounced this act of vengeance, emphasizing this bleeding wound in the nation's recent history. The poet thus ultimately won over the statesman. In this regard, Kocbek remained indebted to the legacy of Prešeren: only after losing direct access to the mechanisms of power and becoming a dissident was Kocbek able to tell the full truth.

This conflict—in many ways a reflection of the old antagonistic tension between liberalism and Roman Catholic clericalism, the two major mental and political paradigms in modern Slovenian history—has served as a difficult yet unavoidable topic for many writers. One of the most comprehensive contemporary novels reflecting this conflict is *The Great Bear* by Miloš Mikeln (b.1930), an epic spanning the entire twentieth century through the lives of two related, yet bitterly opposed, Slovenian families.

LITERARY IDIOMS AND POLITICAL DISSENT

Although Edvard Kocbek was widely acclaimed and enjoyed the support of many international writers, no fame could help him escape the fate of internal exile which denied him publishing opportunities and public contact with his readership. But seeds of resistance to the communist regime had been planted. Jože Udovič (1912–1962), a veteran of resistance and a highly esteemed senior poet, wrote before the Second World War, although most of his work saw publication only after the war's conclusion. Udovič wrote his poems in almost pathological isolation from readers and critics alike, a direct result of his disillusion with communist politics. Udovič rejected most of the literary awards, did not appear at official functions, and declined interviews. Such was his way of saying, "No, thank you!" to political intrusions. In his poems, however, Udovič created a moving world of gradual disintegration of romantic subjects and a retreat from the ideal of beauty, which remained an idealized Ithaca even though the poet was aware that it was only a "mirror of dreams."

The Yugoslav political break with Moscow in 1948 spelled the end of literature which submissively celebrated revolutionary accomplishments. 1953 saw the publication of the first book of lyrical poems that stood above the obligatory social-realist aesthetics. Of the poets who rehabilitated deeply personal voices in the tiny volume *Poems of Four Poets*, Kajetan Kovič (b.1931) commanded the most respect. His was an original vision of darkness and bitterness that drew upon two sources: resigned yet not desperate confrontation with the war generation's legacy of death and an Orphean motif that gave credence to the poet as a voice of historical truth and redemption.

The late fifties and the early sixties were periods of creative eruption. New independent literary journals were established: *Beseda* (The Word), *Revija 57* (Review 57), and *Perspektive* (Perspectives). The first poetry books by major authors Dane Zajc (b.1929) and Veno Taufer (b.1933) appeared in private editions because of political obstruction by the authorities, but literature continued to gain more freedom. The vision of death and the metaphysical void as a wartime legacy were given existentialist grounding in the generation of writers inspired by the re-emerging modernist consciousness.

Diverse aesthetic attitudes that sprang up from this long-awaited modernist turn in Slovenian letters are perhaps best represented by Andrej Hieng (b.1925) and Lojze Kovačič (b.1928). Hieng attracted attention with his minute psychological studies of the charms and decay of the individual mind, while Kovačič focused on largely autobiographical conditions in the life of an outsider. In addition, repression-savvy poets like Dane Zajc, Veno Taufer and Gregor Strniša considerably expanded the possibilities of modern writing.

The mythological poetry of Gregor Strniša (1930–1987) elevated the imagination of his time to the point where heaven meets hell. Embedded in a narrative of cold description replete with mythical creatures and fairy tales, the world in Strniša's poetry was perceived as a kingdom of dark, cruel, and mysterious forces. Strniša's poems bring out two relevant themes: first, that everyday life is the greatest mystery and second, that loneliness is not merely the absence of others but a life among people who do not understand what one is saying. This was an excellent poetic definition of the historical condition of the Slovenians.

Social reality buttressed such dark visions. The colorful horizons of postwar optimism turned in the early sixties into faded photographs in an historical album. Heaven had not descended to earth as was predicted from the communists' loudspeakers; happiness and progress asserted their presence only in official rhetoric. The pursuit of truth and vision was carried out in literary works, not in political speeches.

The secret agents of the regime, "experts of metaphors," to borrow Drago Jančar's phrase, knew that writers enjoyed alarmingly wide support among the common people. Literary magazines, those strongholds of independent intellect, published increasingly biting criticism of corruption and political paralysis. This process of growing dissent culminated in 1964 in massive popular protests. Many attended literary gatherings, university campuses were boiling, night after night poets read their works to enthusiastic audiences of students. They demanded change. The panic-stricken authorities organized duped workers to protest against artists and intellectuals during a theater performance of the play *The Greenhouse*, which ridiculed leading politicians. The play was written by Marjan Rožanc (1930–1990), a budding playwright and literary trouble-maker who later became arguably the best essayist in the country.

Communist *apparatchiks* were compelled to make an example of someone associated with the leading cultural magazine, *Perspektive*, which provided intellectual support for dissent and critically unmasked one communist myth after another. They arrested Tomaž Šalamun (b.1941), an editor of the magazine and a young poet who blasphemously rewrote canonized patriotic poems, thus calling into question the hypocrisy of the regime. Šalamun's most threatening quality seemed to be the fact that the party-line education which was systematically injected into the resigned population had so completely failed with him: equipped with his talent for poetic absurdity, irony and playfulness, Šalamun declared, not unlike his spiritual godfather Arthur Rimbaud, that all dogmatic tradition is the "game of countless idiotic generations."

While Šalamun was soon allowed to leave prison, another *Perspektive* writer, social philosopher Jože Pučnik (b.1932), remained there for years and was, following his release, forced to emigrate. Pučnik, an uncompromising critic of the regime, returned from his German exile only after the democratic elections in 1989 and helped establish a social democratic party.

The magazine was censored and ultimately suspended in 1964. Many writers and cultural critics who today hold leading positions in academic, intellectual, artistic, and even political life in Slovenia, gathered around this magazine. With the benefit of hindsight, one can claim that for Slovenian culture the year 1964 and the far-reaching consequences of civil disobedience and political dissent not only represented a harbinger of May of 1968, but also gave shape to the national dissident imagination in the decades that followed.

Between Solidarity and Solitude

1964 was followed by an era of renewed Stalinist repression, which ran strongly until the end of the seventies. Intellectuals and writers were silenced or exiled. A short intermezzo in 1971, when students occupied the University of Ljubljana for several weeks, was not long enough to recharge the batteries of moral revolt. After the students' defeat, a retreat into the intimate world seemed to be the only solution. The poets baptized by fire during the occupation of the university, notably Boris A. Novak (b.1953), Milan Dekleva (b.1946), and Milan Jesih (b.1950)—who was brought to court because of his participation in literary readings of protest—had defeat etched into their hearts. Censorship became more strict, many writers could not publish, few were employed. Social marginalization was the order of the day.

Writers, however, did not forget that "if you do not deal with politics, politics deals with you," as Czech philosopher Karel Kosik shrewdly noted. Instead of conforming to the standards of social life, writers continued to whisper of a world inside their minds bearing witness to "the minimal self." Alienation from external reality inevitably led the writers of the seventies to rediscover "language as the house of being," as Heidegger would have it.

They explored the limits of lyrical and narrative technique, the vertigo of linguistic possibilities, and the exodus of the coherent plot-line. In these works irony and poetic wise-cracking were employed as protection against, not as a challenge to, external reality. This process may be seen, for example, in the detached fiction of Rudi Šeligo (b.1935), who was inspired by the cool descriptions in the French *nouveau roman*. He later changed course, writing a series of politically critical and very popular theatrical plays during the eighties.

The writer's solitude in the seventies, however, became a central moral principle: resistance was passively expressed through non-involvement in the officially-dictated cultural and political life. While the poetics of linguistic exploration gave an impetus to the postmodernist writers who emerged in the eighties, many luminous authors of the seventies remained trapped in increasingly self-referential loops of brooding textuality.

One of the few writers who did not succumb to this aestheticist temptation was Vitomil Zupan (1914–1987). A notorious *bon vivant*, a boxer, a ski-instructor and a womanizer, Zupan was a prolific writer in every genre. His path diverges from most others in Slovenian literary history, for Zupan's was a life of constant pursuit of ultimate sensations and border-line experiences. Zupan's literary output is enormous by any standard and so is his presence in contemporary Slovenian fiction. Zupan, the adored and feared *enfant terrible* of Slovenian letters, fought with the partisans against Nazis yet was never a communist. Guided instead by a desire for national liberty and personal freedom, he collided with the authorities after the Second World War and was put in prison, where he managed to produce moving testimonies to the endurance of the spirit and the inmates' resourcefulness. While political considerations delayed the publication of some of his work, Zupan's writing life nonetheless represents a rare example of work and biography as an inspiring "chronicle of scandals." In his best work, Zupan attempted to marry introspective existential meditations on the grand issues of life, death, and human transience with a fast-paced narrative that smacked of adventure novels. His later writing is suffused with autobiographical elements, and he did not shy away from openly and graphically addressing the nature of carnal desire, erotic drive, and sexual instinct.

After ten years of literary retreat, public repression, and closed public space, the patience of intellectuals wore thin. The early eighties saw the launching of a new magazine whose very name reveals the manner in which it tried to open public debate: *Nova revija* (The New Review). Not incidentally, several prominent ministers of the independent nation-state in 1991 were recruited from the group of dissident writers and human rights activists who gathered around this important cultural publication. This circle was joined by certain writers who came of age in the seventies, having traveled all the way from harmless linguistic "exercises in style" to the depths of existence and moral need for "life in truth" (Václav Havel). Once dwellers in the ivory towers of textuality, they were transformed into relevant actors in the arena of life. Many, notably the leading formalist poet Boris A. Novak, became radically involved in civil disobedience through such socially marginal, yet morally potent, organizations as the Slovenian Writers' Association and P.E.N. Center.

The poems, novels, testimonies and short stories that writers managed to publish, despite tacit censorship, gradually peeled off layers of lies. The horrors of Titoism, a political system that was much admired among the Western leftist intellectuals, was laid bare, and the truth about *Goli otok* (The Naked Island)—the Yugoslav Gulag that swallowed many dissidents and opponents of the regime—was finally made public. Writers were again at the fore. The communist regime gradually lost ground. In the late eighties, writers joined forces with independent sociologists to challenge the system by writing a proposal for a new constitution. In keeping with long-honored tradition, the writers acted on behalf of the politicians.

In the larger frame of the Yugoslav federation, Serbian appetites, which had been growing since the mid-eighties, posed a tangible threat to the other Yugoslav nations. Serbs usurped the federal administration, illegally appropriated more than half of the hard currency reserves of the federal bank, attempted to alter the national literary curriculum in favor of Serbian authors, and imposed apartheid on ethnic Albanians in the southern province of Kosovo. Slovenia had to choose between two alternatives: remain under the heel of corrupt communist authorities in Belgrade, who were openly flexing their muscles, or establish an independent state.

It was again writers who pushed popular revolt past the point of no return. Following passionate public debates, writers led a group of dissidents and members of the democratic opposition in drafting the declaration of Slovenian independence. It won immediate support with the public. Stimulated by such actions, even Slovenian communists mustered enough political instinct and courage to resist the centralist government. After a public referendum demonstrated by an overwhelming margin the wish of the Slovenian people to live in a free Slovenia, the independent nation-state was declared. Poets, writers and their readers celebrated.

By the end of the eighties, pressing political and state-building concerns no longer required the use of Aesopian language and cryptic poetic metaphors. The new conditions particularly appealed to poets and writers who came of age in the eighties. While older colleagues spearheaded the struggle for an independent nation-state, the nascent generation felt somewhat left aside in these political concerns. Consequently, their inclination was to explore the formal and metaphysical possibilities of imagination, and they refused to view literature as the one and only platform from which political opinions could be voiced. Postmodernism in its various manifestations became the slogan of the decade.

Andrej Blatnik (b.1963) is perhaps the most representative prose writer of this international style, which found its home on the pages of the magazine *Literatura*. Established in the eighties, its simple name declares the return of writers' primary concern: literature. Blatnik's short stories are permeated with sophisticated references to other literary works and past narrative strategies, and to the fictional character of the truth itself.

On the other side of the aesthetic spectrum in this decade stands the work of fiction writer Berta Bojetu-Boeta (1946-1997). Her dark, painful and anxious literary account of the suffocating atmosphere is as much the legacy of past political and personal bondage as it is its disturbingly beautiful portrait.

While Bojetu-Boeta's fiction is obsessed with the experience of psychological and physical suffering, the widely translated work of Drago Jančar (b.1948) is rich both in subject matter and narrative techniques. Jančar spent a few months in jail on fabricated charges of "anti-communist propaganda" in the seventies. Like many of his generation, Jančar is unmistakably political in his social instincts and penetrating essays. With existential courage and stylistic dexterity, Jančar does not recoil from political issues in his literary work. In his novels and short stories, he uses a variety of hermetic, testimonial, realist and postmodernist devices to better focus on the "terror of history" and the chances for survival the individual may have in the great grinding machine of homogenization, including the corporate and technological mindsets of contemporary Western societies.

When discussing Slovenian literature in the eighties in the context of a healthy distance from politics, it is nevertheless mandatory to emphasize that the long-called-for separation of politics and literature was not meant to give birth to some myopic version of *l'art pour l'art*. Inasmuch as moral habits are embedded in the intricacies of historic allegory and allusion, the urge to stress them is beside the point, argued young Slovenian postmodern writers. A recognition of history and its discontents is always present, since the writer's historical sensibility and responsibility make their way into the work by virtue of language, a shared stock of metaphors, and cultural tradition.

Arguing for a critical separation of civil engagement and autonomous writing—many years overdue in Central and Eastern Europe as a whole— young writers championed a distinct attitude: a writer can only aspire to be a witness of his or her times if the writing itself is free of any external prescriptions. The young writers of the eighties hence espoused a kind of Joycean *non serviam* to the cause of Slovenian independence. I hasten to add that their civic and moral responsibility was, in accord with the best Slovenian tradition of intellectuals *qua* politicians, articulated outside the literary medium, notably in newspaper columns and other public forums. This was a novel approach to literature in a Central and Eastern Europe customarily associated with the noble mind, which is, as Czeslaw Milosz once remarked, of no particular use to literature. Slovenian postmodernists, in other words, believed that a creative self can only bloom beyond the divisions of progressive vs. conservative.

The views of the young generation aptly correspond with the radically changed cultural situation. The writers' historical mission is, it seems, for the most part accomplished. Slovenians now have a nation-state. Prešeren's toast to freedom may now be sung in a free country, not clandestinely but at official functions and, if one wishes, at the top of one's lungs. New social and historical conditions care less for imaginative writing and more for business, advancing the commerce of goods rather than the commerce of ideas. Literature in this social nexus no longer represents the privileged forum of truth, justice and beauty and thus, by extension, of national identity. The role of the writer as revered shaman and spokesman for the people, recounting the stories of historical taboos, suppressed memory, individual solitude and social resistance, is in all likelihood over. The curtains are being drawn, the performance of writers as decisive actors in the public arena is slowly coming to an end.

The social meaning of the writer's vocation has irreversibly changed. It is commonly believed that if a writer no longer runs the risk of going to prison for what he publishes, then his words lack the moral weight they carried before. While the writers' search for the truth about *ex Oriente lux*, "the light from the East," is answered by readers' craving for *ex Occidente luxus*, "luxurious goods from the West," writers recognize that a political theme alone no longer provides a desired historical and aesthetic alibi. This helps explain why there have been surprisingly few literary works published so far that deal comprehensively with the post-independence period. While the most important historical threshold in the life of a nation etched itself permanently into Slovenian collective memory, it still awaits its poet. In his absence, sophisticated and courageous journalists such as Spomenka Hribar (b.1941), Ervin Hladnik-Milharčič (b.1954) and Ivo Štandeker (1961–1992), who was killed by a Serbian sniper while on assignment in Bosnia, have done their share of work in the increasingly popular genre of "creative non-fiction."

By many accounts, burning public issues no longer command the total attention of the population, which is increasingly turning toward private, intimate pursuits. Grand metaphysical and political ideas of the nation, community and history, attractive as they were because of their all-encompassing values, are being gradually replaced by human-size concerns. Hence the writer's life has ceased to be, in a radical and traumatic way, intertwined with that of the nation. The hereditary syndrome of Prešeren, whose work could mobilize the entire community, may have reached an impasse, revealing the limits of what it can "make happen" for the contemporary Slovenian mind. Writers now face a challenge of a radically different kind: how to honor the cultural tradition that nurtured them and at the same time to speak movingly about the time of independence which ushered in the post-communist epoch with its shifting values and symbols, and with its redefinition of the writers' profession. This is an epoch that seems to require an entirely different language and aesthetic style.

To be sure, this is not a unique Slovenian predicament. It is experienced all over Central and Eastern Europe where writers no longer occupy the privileged position of political visionaries. The pursuit of artistically coherent and morally lucid writing which oscillates between historical amnesia and the indiscriminate amnesty for past traumas thus stands at the center of contemporary Slovenian writing. The literary consequences of this are bound to help determine the spirit of the time at the turn of the troubled millennium.

Melancholy Meditations
on Slovenian Literature

Andrej Inkret

It would be impossible for this essay to be anything other than a brief sim-
plification of some of the characteristics of Slovenian literature, intended
chiefly for the interested non-Slovenian. Slovenian literature is almost
unknown beyond the region encompassed by the language, the historical
exceptions of individual writers notwithstanding.

However, the fact is that none of the poets and other men of letters who
have contributed to the almost two hundred years of Slovenian lay literature, from the Enlightenment and Romanticism onwards, has ever managed
to break through in a decisive way to the general consciousness of European
literary and spiritual tradition. Presently, all have remained only and solely
Slovenian writers. Even those celebrated poets and writers evaluated by literary history and current criticism in Slovenian have only experienced brief,
sporadic, more or less cursory translations into other languages. But though
this is true, some of these, in their ingenuity and appeal and—if one wishes—in the universality of their artistic vision, are by all measures up to the
standard of so-called European literature. While the European canon, as it
were, is extremely approximate and in some profound, historical sense arbitrary, Slovenian literature has never had any influence upon it. This fact is
bemoaned, be it silently or publicly, by all of us here who have dealings of

any kind with literature in Slovenian, especially since literature historically has enjoyed a special national and social regard. Also known only too well to us is that the history of literature in Europe is, in both essential ideas and stylistic parameters, the history of Slovenian literature. Sadly, literature in Slovenia has lived in this one-way communication with the European literary and spiritual complex for too long.

Early utilitarian and religious Slovenian literature had its beginnings in the Protestant Reformation of the sixteenth century. However, the first truly literary texts in Slovenian came into being only two centuries later. Though Slovenian literature has been bound by its language borders, it has never been insular or claustrophobic and only rarely has shown flashes of xenophobia. To paraphrase Wittgenstein: the boundaries of one's language are not the boundaries of one's world. This has been profoundly true in Slovenia.

Ideas and stimulation from Europe have been used openly and without prejudice in Slovenian literature, but within its own geographical, historical and spiritual context. However, Slovenian ideas have had less impact on European letters. Considering the special national and historical fate of Slovenians, this was objectively impossible for a long period; at the same time perhaps, it was also undesired. Revealing its own main task and significance as inner witness to the specific actualities and authentic perspectives of the Slovenian community, Slovenian literature devoted itself to its own forms with particular perseverance and intensity.

It is precisely literature that has in some profound, subtle sense safeguarded the Slovenian community from the imperialistic appetites of stronger and more expansive nations in the region. Numerically small, with historical, geographical and political deficiencies, the Slovenian nation has often participated in various pan- and south-Slavic movements (largely in the interest of self-preservation), some of which have originated here. Other ideas—particularly some generated after WWII—have suggested a gradual dissolution of national identity into some kind of international working-class ethos that would become the sole social reality in some approximated communistic future. Ideas about the abolition of the Slovenian nation are frequent and relatively broad in dimension. It is unnecessary to emphasize that ultimately it all has the same demoralizing effect, whether these ideas appear under the name of some universal liberating or eschatological vision or originate from some political party appetite. Sooner or later their end result is the same. From this modern social, political and ultimately economic point of view, the Slovenian national existence is marginal, unproductive and perhaps even irrelevant.

As the principal expression of the Slovenian language, Slovenian literature was for a long time, perhaps right up to the end of the First World War, the primary, fundamental and most representative form that Slovenians had of a legitimate national community. It was as well an important substitute for the historical State that Slovenia was often unable to secure for itself. It was certainly the chief generator of the Slovenian collective consciousness in the ethnic and psychological sense. Literature was the highest national institution and authority. Ironically, biographies of the most important Slovenian writers as a rule don't sell well because Slovenians almost always detect their significance only posthumously.

It is therefore possible to say that we Slovenians are in some way a literary nation, or that we value our literary tradition. For a longer period the national question in Slovenia was also the literary one, and the history of the Slovenian national spirit can be seen in the history of Slovenian literature. Even today the anachronistic idea of literature's constitutive, redemptive character and mission can still be found in Slovenia. And Slovenian writers are still obliged to address every social and moral deficiency of the prevailing political power through their letters. For here in Slovenian lands, literature has been our lifeblood.

The most important works in Slovenian literature stand up even to so-called European standards. Slovenian literature can never, ever be comprehended as an instrument administered by some *a priori* religious or political idea, as the manifestation of some nationalistic will. In fact, the opposite is true: Slovenia's celebrated works contain tales of original yet universal human problems. National identification (descent, language, political or social affiliation and spiritual tradition) is but one of the elements that make up humanness in Slovenian literature.

Frequently in literature and poetry, that vulgar, nationalistic ideology asserting that man's essence is defined and determined by his group association, is expressed: "I am a man in as much as I am Slovenian, or a German or a Turk." This tradition is completely foreign to Slovenians. It is clear in our literature that the metaphysical starting point of every valid literary work or poem is completely the opposite. Only in my essential humanness is my Slovenian essence also realized. In other words, my existential truth is not formed solely by the truth of my Sloveneness, however binding and fateful this may be for me. There is always a difference between my existential soul and my Slovenian being.

This difference is due to man's irreducible humanness, at its living and individual core constituting the consciousness of boundless liberty, as well as the irrevocable notion of end and death. Similarly, human affiliation to collective traditions and cultures, to this or that form of social or historical power or institution, where freedom and death lose their status as man's ontological definitions, decisively alters ideas and ideologies, will and power. It is here, in this gap, that the space opens up into which literature or artistic articulation of the complex truths of the human world can flourish.

As I see it, the authentic Slovenian dimension of literature lies in its willingness to wholly address existing human problems. Slovenian literature is, of course, essentially defined by its national element, and expressed in its own language (the sole instrument of every literature). And although the question of the nation is indistinguishably linked to that of literature, the fact is that Slovenian literature knows precisely that man does not belong genetically to a particular nation but simply regards it as a system of arbitrary cultural and social values. Such categorization is, of course, based on free, open, critical decisions, which can be radical and offer writers the unique opportunity to stand outside social boundaries. Also ultimately true is that among Slovenian writers who have made their name, there are none who has abandoned Slovenian to write in any other language. Though other languages have always had a place in Slovenia—out of necessity and pragmatism—these only appear sporadically in our literature and rarely solely on account of deficiencies in the Slovenian tongue. The two hundred years of Slovenian literature is testament to writers here that their fated Slovenian essence is more powerful than the original political and military strides that made Slovenia a modern nation. Or can it be that freedom reveals itself in their persistent, stubborn and certainly irrational (and impractical) fidelity to the Slovenian language, in the narrow confines of which they enclose themselves? Can it be that this is the only language in which they can possibly write?

Translated by Anne Čeh.

On Poetry

Edvard Kocbek

A human being calculates the value of his life in two ways: first, through a rational understanding of reality, that is, through a systematic and practically organized knowledge of it; and second, by experiencing reality as a spontaneous and liberating overcoming of its logic. We call the first activity science, the second, art.

The purpose of science is to discover and organize the cognition of basic laws, with the help of various techniques, to improve conditions of our risky lives. Science progresses by moving from one relative truth to another, and it can never reach global comprehension. The position of science is agnostic, spiritually neutral; it strives for the most secure and objective identification of things in achieved truths. It must ignore all questions of ethical and ultimate concepts, because science provides only a partial view of human wholeness and our deepest curiosity, which is of a metaphysical nature. These matters are left to humankind's second type of curiosity, which does not lie in causal logic and carefully-bound examination. They are left to art.

For art we should say poeticism, and while poeticism is an essential element of visual art and music, it is first and foremost the essence of verbal expression. Poeticism is the all-encompassing, munificent and salvatory experience of everything that is. It is thus alogical and non-causal, as well as a complete and ecstatic comprehension of truth as a giving over to being and the liberation of the soul. Poeticism is proof that, despite all the achievements of science and victories of technology, we live in a world of unpredictable and incalculable becoming, a world of fate and mystery that leaves us with a feeling of constant insufficiency. If science strives for identification, poetry lusts after authentification. To be authentic is to sense the center of the universe and from that center to pronounce complete experience. If science is the systematic organization of exact laws concerning dead and living matter, then poeticism is the irrepressible and joyful embrace of imaginative play with the most varied elements of fate, with the goal of using them to create a holistic vision.

In the conditions of everyday life, there is not and should not be an opposition between scientific and artistic truth such that the values of one cancel out the values of the other. On the contrary, it appears that both—each in its own way—have a role to play in the process of overcoming the self, one through reason, the other through imagination. We call this process of overcoming creativity, and what interests us here, most of all, is artistic creativity, in which we would like to discover the central movement of poetic activity.

As far back as we can remember, humankind has been aware of the possibility of qualitative improvement. A desire to overcome the present order of things through imaginative intensity is inborn in human beings. The most interesting fact is that in this imaginative process we have a strong inner conviction that only in the realm of fantasy can we move from reality to authentic truth. At times we are overcome with the sensation that only through this inventive method can we satisfy our desire for the wholeness of things or phenomena. The consciousness of humankind is so organized that everything that is given is given only partially, and thus we need to supplement each partial given through the ecstatic intensity of our soul. The imaginative capability is invisible, but its spontaneous appearance in human spiritual life shows that it is a necessary and actual phenomenon. Without it, we cannot imagine the qualitative change that is the essence of creativity. We will see that only in poetry is creativity a category of pure, intensive and whole labor.

Long ago humankind identified the origins of poetry with the myth that speaks of the loss of wholeness. This ur-history of humankind encompasses various explanations of humanity's loss of freedom. The myth says that the original human being was exiled from a paradise of happiness due to some fatal transgression. Exile mutilated the original human, making him merely part of the whole; afterwards only nostalgic memories and longing confirm its existence. That exile marked the beginning of a psychological straining toward wholeness and unity for the human being. Thus, poetry is a yearning for lost harmony. With acute hearing in the cosmic and fateful atmosphere, a poet searches for the separated notes of a lost harmony: sounds, words, sentences, melodies, and with these meter, rhythm, verse and rhyme. This poetic game takes place in all peoples and at all times, except that its nostalgic content changes. Thus, from time to time, out of the mass of humankind a poet arises who, mired as we are in depressing moments of emptiness, estrangement and desperation, lights our way with the god-like strength of his wholeness and universality so that we experience moments of immortality. Every true artist stands in opposition to death—our most fateful border—as a ruler over the tricks of fate. He looks death courageously in the eyes, as did Kafka when he said, "All the best things I have written come from the capability that they will allow me to die satisfied." Whoever achieves poetic transcendence obtains power over death itself.

Poetry is the guarantor of authenticity in music, as it is in painting and dance. But its truest medium is the word. For the poet, poetry is linked to language, that same linguistic material through which he became human and through whose words, as the carriers of meaning, he first made contact with the mysteries of the world when he was still being caressed by his mother or playing with his earliest friend. The word is thus given to the poet at the beginning; it is present in his cradle, which is why verbal poetry is the most natural of all the arts. The poet Francis Ponge says that through verbal play, every person is guided toward the wisdom of nature and the justice of things. Through words, the most broadly-shared vehicles of expression, poetry should be at home in every person, says the linguist Chomsky, since language is not limited to practical communication but also serves as the means for free thought and original self-expression. Language is unquestionably the most humanizing faculty of man and the highest achievement of his development; and the highest achievement of language is not logical thought but rather poetry, asserts Ivan Svitak. Thus the lyric contains the highest concentration of humanity: it is the acme of human potential.

A poem does not accommodate itself to habit, nor is it subordinate to any human order. It expresses itself according to its own free will, and it reveals itself without declarations or preparation. A poem is thus revelation and grace. Absolute chance. Frightening lawlessness. And while in the depths, invisible cohesive forces bring it into being, pushing it toward a meeting with our earliest memories and presentiments in order to produce a chaotic eruption. A person experiences this quiet torment day and night, slowly mulls it over, turns it over in his hands, thinks about it, falls asleep with this torment and wakes with it, endures it for many days and nights, becomes blind and deaf to the world, begins to drag it around as if he were a pregnant animal going into labor. You breathe ever harder, anchored only in the unknown depths of things, knowing nothing of the banal world, its vegetativeness, its rules and laws. But then relief begins, for you look around and find a word, and you connect it to another, still unrecognized, then to a third. A germ of meaning appears, the melody of a sentence takes shape, and thus you release something that comes as a liberation. And behold, here is a newborn being. Your heart beats with joy. It is filled in and rounded off, a body among other bodies. Now all that remains is the external side, the polishing, the first oral presentation. All that remains is to give thanks with closed eyes, for the conception and birth simultaneously. Finally, you are left with a melancholy mood, as is usually the case after making love.

We possess various definitions of poeticism. I will note a few here: poetry is an appeal to mankind to leave its vegetative state and move to the heights of loftier values; poetry is a vision of the truth and allows for greater and deeper revelations than can be provided by rational knowledge; poetry is the sovereignty of the human spirit which is based not on rational but on artistic truth; poetry is the creative expression of a cosmic and portentous wholeness; poetry is the ecstatic perception of materiality as infinitely rich meaning; poetry is the magical revelation of human capability; poetry is the means by which man becomes reconciled with the world, secures himself against it, and mystically rises above it; poeticism is man's sensation of freely controlling the world; poetry is linguistic adventure that uncovers unknown and unknowable qualities in human beings and the universe; poetry is divination on the border of the world of dreams and the world of reality; poetry is the abjuration of evil and the appellation of good, the exorcism of malevolent spirits and the conjuring of good ones.

Let us look more closely at how poetry expresses its paradoxical meaning. Most importantly, we should note that words in poetic use become polyvalent, i.e., take on multiple meanings. Even the most overused word becomes polyvalent in a poetic context. In general, when speaking of poetic use, we're dealing with two major, competing concepts: the semantic and the structural meanings of a word. The former is rooted in the gigantic lexical richness of each language; the latter is built on the formal and functional definitions of logical syntax. The greatest abundance of meanings arises in semantic syntax: its space opens out to such strong and free atmospheric changes that in its aura words take on a broad gamut of meanings. Three basic experiential categories influence the meaning of words most strongly: vital ecstasy, tragedy, and universal eroticism.

Whenever we look at a poem *in toto*, the first thing we recognize is that a poem implies a complete transformation of meaning. In the face of this fact, a person might say that a poem has nothing to do with everyday reality, that poetic text is not as true as other everyday texts such as pamphlets, legal documents, scientific reports, or newspaper articles. None of these texts is poetic. This is not to say that a poetic text is actually less valuable or that it is an expression of a higher truth; rather, it means that a poetic text is based on a qualitatively different foundation than so-called realistic texts. The basic language of the two types of texts is identical. The difference is in the subtle and disciplined choice of words. In an artistically effective text, each word is in its proper place, none is superfluous, nothing is missing. The essence of poetic thought is also the unsubstitutability of words. A poem is distinguished by the tension between provocation and risk, between expression and silence, in short, between content and form, between the sincerity of content and the integrity of form.

For some poets, this tendency goes to such lengths that they are silent more than they speak. The poet Günther Eich says: "I sense some kinship between a poem and Chinese writing. In the latter, meaning is concentrated, because the Chinese do not render words alphabetically or phonetically but through pictures, that is, in maximally gnomic fashion." This is why we can speak of so-called gaps in poetic texts. A realistic or documentary text must be filled with information, such that at every moment and in every place we can verify whether the text is adequate to its purpose. Artistic texts do not recognize such definite and rigidly organized structures. The essential individuality of a poem is predicated on its willingness to break up the flow of its narrative or to jump around within it. We say that poetry is characterized by empty spaces. This we could identify as the poet's creative freedom. We are not speaking here merely about the elimination of everything superfluous in a poem; we are speaking about an artistic device which invites or compels the reader to fill in the information gaps in a poem with his own inventions. By its very nature a poem is an invitation to the re-creation of poetic language and its fateful history. Through these lacunae in a poem, a poet leads the reader into unknown lands, as if the poem were a guidebook; sooner or later some kind of congruity is reached between the markings on a map and one's actual path through an unknown city. Here, too, although a poem offers certain documentary lines, it can preserve its fictiveness only if it contains or simulates a pseudo-documentary authenticity, since a work of art in its development is an imagined reality despite the fact that it is constructed of elements of first-order reality. With every sentence we read, our perception of distorted reality becomes fuller, although, paradoxically, it also becomes more open. Whenever a literary work coalesces into an authentic whole in the reader's imagination, only one of its potential variants is activated.

Literary art is thus not identical with truth. Poetry is only a challenge or the answer to a challenge. Despite the fact that it does not have anything to do with unmediated or real events, and despite the fact that the author has no such intention, a true work of art always contains newly-prepared historical power. At any time and place, its contents can be understood as an answer to the most oft-posed questions. This disturbing role of poetry has been beautifully described by the German literary theorist Dieter Wellershoff. Musing on the difference between literature and life, he began by comparing literature to the new technology of the simulator. He took this metaphor from new techniques of space flight, which deals with new and unexpected experiences by modeling them in a special training room. There, astronauts can adapt to weightlessness, train to control themselves, and thereby become acquainted with all phases of their upcoming flight. This system of simulation, in his analogy, can help us understand poetry. Poetry for him is a simulator for the exercise of the mind, a playground for inventive manipulation, in which authors as well as readers can go beyond their practical experience without subjecting themselves to any real-world risk.

I believe this comparison is useful. Indeed, literature is not reality, nor does it express verifiable impressions of reality. Instead, it provides propositions or points of view on life situations to which we have never been exposed but which are nonetheless possible. We certainly can't adapt ourselves to situations of mental manipulation the way an astronaut in a simulator can: his movements are strictly limited, while a poet is freer. Thus, the problem with this analogy is that a poet's position allows for far greater and freer manipulation. In other words, the goal of poetry is not the exact modeling of some situation, but rather a constant and irrepressible investigation of the possibilities of mental play. The purpose of human literary creativity is precisely in its exploitation of the unlimited possibilities for variation and fantasy. The writer and poet undoubtedly also see a very real picture of the human being in society, history, nature, and in himself. That is why many of these fantasies are quite serious. Whenever, in their desires or thoughts, writers examine happiness and unhappiness, good and evil, they must risk as much as the astronaut when he leaves the simulator. The difference is that the writer or poet cannot use any patterns worked out in advance.

A formal and a sensual instinct rule over mankind and the world. The sensual instinct expresses a need for sensual experiments with matter; the formal instinct expresses a psychological need for measure and abstraction. The tension between them leads to a dangerously antagonistic relationship. We can bridge this dangerous gap only by turning to a third instinct, the instinct for free play. To this instinct is given the potential to overcome the antagonistic forces within us and in our activity. This third instinct operates especially in the realm of art, the realm truly designed for the triumph of play. No other arena of life can provide us with as much freedom as we can achieve through artistic creation. In these musings on poetry we discover its basic meaning. Art is the play of the human gambler who stakes everything, even freedom itself, although in so doing he does not in any way impinge on the freedom of others. Science and technology understand and transform the world, lengthen human life, raise the standard of living, eliminate sickness and poverty. All of this is absolutely necessary. But all of this means nothing more than the creation of crucial initial conditions. The most important and necessary things follow from this, for they do nothing more than create the space for that redemptive play we call freedom. I achieve liberation whenever I do battle with instinctual and abstract terrors not only in legal and ethical situations but also in my commitment to my own play. In play, my decisions are most sovereign and I am in the highest state of imagination, a state in which I constantly give myself over to new challenges and new victories. In the authentic space of creation, I am most true to my humanity. In this space my responsibility is greatest because it is confronted with deeds of a magnitude greater than the legal or the moral. In poetic creation I am free for, but not from, anything. In this space my free decisions are an answer to all of life's truth.

In this space, we recognize that man is greater than himself. In this space, the belief that we live only for production, accumulation, manipulation and advantage loses its power. It is replaced by the recognition that true humanity is based on ecstasy, on unquantifiable wholeness, and on playful freedom. A human being is not an object to be controlled but a subject who can conquer and outgrow himself. That is the sovereign word of poetry.

Translated by Andrew Wachtel.

Excerpts from
Pilgrim Among the Shadows

Boris Pahor

Once again the medics were the only ones with a plan amid the confusion: we determined that one building should be the hospital, or rather a haven for the emaciated and dying. It is possible that this decision was dictated by our own instinct for self-preservation, but if so, it had nothing to do with any law of the survival of the fittest. Concern for one's fellow man needn't derive from selfish calculation or from altruism, for that matter. It may be an organic need, like breathing or the exercise of thought. It may have to do with self-preservation only in the sense that work is above all a way for man to escape himself. Despite all the deaths there was still quite a crowd, and we had responsibilities, tasks: the relocation of bunk beds from room to room, the search for mattresses, the division of rooms into wards for edema, for gangrene, for dysentery, and of course for the sticklike mummies standing motionless in the corridors, oblivious to all around them. And then the disposition of the bodies and their proper burial. Lying still was the best medicine, in lieu of all the medicine we didn't have, the best even when the body was beyond hope, for it was the most appropriate position for that gentle slide into emptiness, when veins and muscles had dried into thongs of barely clinging vine that no longer transmitted pain. Worse even than the lack of food—some of our patients turning their eyes toward me as hatchlings turn their beaks, especially the ones with edema, who indeed resembled hatchlings with their swollen, sausagelike eyelids—was the complete absence of all the ritual appurtenances of the medical art. All we had were paper bandages, alcohol, and big ampules of glucose. No one knew why there had been so much of the sugar solution in the SS clinic at Harzungen. We also had two-centiliter ampules of Coramine, which was useless for treating edema or dysentery. And thermometers. The thermometers alone created a clinical atmosphere, weaving an unseen web of silence and common cause between the hastily arranged bunks and the medics until darkness began to creep through the windows. But by then everything had been organized, the first two bodies had even been laid along the side wall of the building. When I leaned out the window of my "ward" and saw them, it struck me that at the end of their odyssey they deserved to have their bones covered with sackcloth. Tomorrow someone would commend them to the earth. Aside from the moans and pleas, the building was peaceful and orderly. This couldn't be said of the other quarters, from which we could hear muffled waves of commotion. Only night subdued the struggles for sleeping space and the search for nonexistent food, leaving the air saturated with a distant rumbling. The horizon was a line of rolling murmurs, the sign of our approaching salvation. By day the rumbling receded to some remote corner of the world. Fear still stirred beneath the surface of our endless tasks. We were, after all, in Bergen-Belsen, and though the camp itself was in the background, this was a place of annihilation, and there was no reason for it to single us out for mercy.

One morning a pack of prisoners ignored a sign with skull and crossbones (what was it there for, anyway?) and went looking for water in a brick shed right across from our building—from the hospital. I noticed them as I went to the window to see how long the row of bodies was getting. Two men had just stepped inside the small building, and the rest scattered when they saw a guard approaching. He was a kid still, with a longish face and dark eyes, skinny in his SS uniform. He didn't speak or shout, he just swore under his breath as he released the safety on his rifle and fired at one of the men as he emerged from the shed carrying a jug of water. The prisoner staggered and fell, and water splashed out as the jug hit the ground. The boy fired again, slowly pulling the trigger. Then he fired at the second man, who had dropped his jug and was hopping on one foot. The boy laughed and once more carefully pulled the trigger. I lost sight of the victim as he tried to escape, the corner of the hospital blocking my view. Judging by the boy's smile as he shouldered his rifle—he had enjoyed this—it could have come out either way. Still entertaining, even if the hopper got away. Then the guard began to curse loudly over the body that lay motionless, and I realized he was a Croat *ustaša*. I felt hollow at the sound of kindred Slavic words spoken in such circumstances, but was also surprised at the daring of our striped comrades. The fact that resistance was still alive though it had long seemed dead was to me proof that the world of the crematoria was finished.

But I had some useful work to do just then, because someone had brought in sulfa tablets. Who knows where or how the busy fingers had found them. Most likely in some veterinary station, because the tablets were as big as bottle tops and I had to break them in quarters, and even then a patient would have a hard time swallowing them. But what counted was that I had sulfa and that now the ritual could proceed, both for the patients and for myself. Another question, how they would benefit from it, for sulfa is no nutrient for dehydrated protoplasm. Along the wall outside, the row of bodies grew. Our building was so filled, even the attic was used. I went upstairs to the attic, I don't know why. Perhaps out of zeal to find more patients with dysentery or edema, or else to break the spell of savagery and indecision by doing something different, or simply from the need a captive feels to walk the perimeter of his captivity. It wasn't the kind of attic where secrets are kept, a hodgepodge of objects as ancient as the cobwebs that wreathe them. There were only huge, heavy beams rising up at angles from floor to ceiling. Zebra-striped people lay on the floor beneath the beams, wedged into each other every which way, and the voices in this tangled mass were foul bubbles escaping from mud. The attic window was open. The cold air that came through cleared away some of the stink, but the bodies had formed a semicircle around the window to avoid the cold. Except for one person who lay right in front of it, alone in the piercing air, swept from the solid human shore and now drifting out to the sea of nothingness. Some impatient stretcher bearer had dumped him there. I was disturbed by the shape of his limbs, the peculiar way they sprawled. It was familiar, the shaved head belonged to Ivanček. Then I saw his bright, lively eyes, which were searching for me. As is always the case in the last stages, the remaining moisture of his body had collected in them, glistening, yet they still preserved the timidity of a young boy whose swashbuckling adventure tales had been replaced by inconceivable images of assembly-line death. While his eyes besieged me, as though they were not only trying to escape death's strait-jacket but also wanted to communicate to me all the fury of his physical being, I once again saw the kind, pleading smile he had as he left Harzungen. Because precisely at the moment we had to walk to the station, fleeing the pincers of eastern and western fronts, precisely at that moment Ivanček received—who knows how—a package from his village in Slovenia. "Beautiful, golden biscuits," he said, holding the parcel in his lap like a young mother awkward with her newborn. It was as though his fam-ily had managed to come to their little boy's rescue in the nick of time, had come all the way from the other side of the world. I suppose he brought me his biscuits because I had given him mess tins of stew left over from the day's corpses, in exchange for which he would bring from the tunnels pieces of wood for the stove. He carried the wood under his shirt so the guards wouldn't see it. But this afternoon he had stuffed his shirt with biscuits and tied a ragged apron tightly around his waist, the blue-and-gray stripes bil-lowing as if they covered some animal. He stroked the shapeless hump, pro-tected it with his hands, as if aware of the sanctity of the provisions his native land had sent him for his final, long ordeal. Now, however, he lay on the floor, alone. "Ivan," I tried to rouse him with the confident voice of peo-ple who imagine they have firm ground beneath their feet, but it came out lame and hollow, and his eyes were right to repulse it. I didn't look into them when I crouched down beside him and put my ear close to his mouth like a mountain climber listening at the edge of the precipice that swallowed his partner. Words came piecemeal, faint, and told me that it was from the golden biscuits he moistened in his mouth that he had slowly drawn life, every day, day after day, for the duration of our aimless wandering in open cattle cars, where he stood without protection against the hard mass of bod-ies pressing up against his shirtfront stuffed with rations, or against the hands that grabbed, the knees that shoved, the feet that trampled until they finally trampled his body to the floor. I knelt over his dehydrated head, powerless to help, nor could I have saved him had I known he was lying on the floor of one of those cars that I walked past so many times when we ban-daged gangrene cases and carried corpses to the two cars nearest the engine. I wouldn't have had anything to give him—but at least he could have had a quiet corner to himself, like Janoš's Pole. I could have broken off the end of an ampule of fructose and poured the sweet liquid in his mouth. Distressed, I ran for a syringe and the large ampules, as if zeal combined with the right ceremonial objects could turn back the clock. That's what we hope for. We hope that kindness will prevail and lives will be saved. This is the innocent, beautiful instinct of our youth, which sometimes survives our youth and lives on stubbornly. I pulled away the faded, stinking striped outer skin to reveal the boy's plucked, cranelike bones. I had seen thousands of such bones, carried dozens to the anteroom of the oven, but in the presence of this body my professional calm vanished. I had tried to save this life with the food of our dead, and it was now leaving me with the good-natured smile of a Slovene boy. I couldn't find a place for the needle between bone and the coarse, thin skin stretched over it. The sunken thigh was unresponsive, and the sugar water ran out of his mouth. He probably couldn't have been helped even if a doctor had injected plasma into his veins. A sudden anxiety came to his eyes, similar to the irritability of old age, and it didn't subside even after I carried him to the quiet of a dark corner. He probably did not know who was laying him down in a military grain bin side by side with other bodies. I went back downstairs, and as I started splitting the huge sulfa tablets, I thought that soon, that very afternoon, Ivanček would be lying in a row with others beneath my window, and this seemed a lesser evil than my defeat, than my silent shame, than my powerlessness. Without faith, machinelike, I halved the huge tablets meant for good-natured horses and that human bodies would therefore resist.

* * *

I see myself hidden in a barracks in the evening, waiting for the watchman to lock the outer door to the abandoned cattle pen. He has no reason to think that anyone would want to spend the night in this soundless preserve. He is not, after all, a guard in the Louvre, with priceless canvases to protect. There are no paintings here that would make anybody's mouth water. I step out of the barracks and stand on the terrace. To my right, darkness and the beak of the gallows; beneath me, striped figures huddled on the narrow strips of level ground all the way down the hillside. The barracks are gone, so there are empty spaces to the sides, yet the rows of figures press as close together as ever to keep warm. They are motionless—shadows in burlap, which hangs from their shoulders as from the prongs of a wooden rake. No one was designated to inspect these rows on the terraces. Only I am there. I know that it is not on my account that they are made to stand there against their will, yet even so I begin to feel guilt. Before I have time to consider the implications of this, Leif appears before me at a long table. Now I see lines of bodies standing naked in the sun, waiting to be examined. A crucial selection. But I was only an interpreter at those selections, I had nothing to do with the final decision. I hurt no one. Ultimately, even Leif's choices depended on the most cursory visual impression—the numbers simply didn't allow for any other method. Then why this icy silence from the formations of prisoners? No, they are not assembled here to judge me. Every night, after the terraces have been cleared of living visitors, they gather to resanctify the ground over which so much summer footwear has walked. They stand silent like orphaned Byzantine saints, gazing defiantly ahead. But someone could at least nod in my direction, acknowledge me. Even if it is a glassy stare of condemnation. Anything would be better than this cold neglect. What is it you think I did wrong? Why do you let me walk past you down the steps like a stranger? Even you, who came from the same block as I? We used to sit together, lie together on the dirt outside the barracks. We pressed our limbs to the earth in hopes that some healing radiation would come from the strata of heavy rock and penetrate our atrophied tissues. Or was mingling with the earth simply an expression of submission, of our desire for final rest, for the silencing of all contradictions and all voices? Our motionlessness was like the waiting of old men, their veins dry, their muscles withered. Except that old men are not so utterly hollow. And yet, on the narrow strip in front of the barracks, we were alert inside, because hunger, until it reaches a certain stage, does not exhaust or mortify; it forces the body into irrational motion, agitated rambling. The greed of the digestive cells is transferred to the ears and eyes, which are on constant, irritated guard to intercept the slightest encouraging noise or reflection. Of course, we knew all too well that no change would come, no surprise, but apparently this alertness itself fulfills some need of the frustrated organism. Take the negotiations over an exchange of bread and cigarettes. All eyes are on a piece of bread the size of a postcard and two fingers thick. It looks like a quarter of an old roofing tile, desiccated and cracked and worn at the edges, because the owner kept it under his shirt to make sure no one stole it at night. The eyes cannot believe that he would relinquish it for a dozen cigarettes; but they do not know the passion of the smoker, the trembling fingers, the working Adam's apple, the rising saliva. All eyes follow the new owner as he presses the piece of furrowed tile to his chest and departs through the crowd to savor each future bite in solitude.

I stand on the steps at the level of our block, in the mountain night, and the prisoners keep silent. Why don't they move? Why don't they call out to me? I know why. It's because of the bread I took from them with cigarettes. I confess my sin. It happened only once, because I never had access to cigarettes again. But that doesn't lessen the crime. I told myself that if I didn't get it, the square piece of bread would find its way into someone else's possession. I vacillated between mercy—to simply give him the cigarettes and appease his smoker's passion—and weakness, my mouth tasting the bread in anticipation. I didn't actually eat the bread until night, though the transaction took place as the day was just beginning. My body was recovering from dysentery, and the mucous membranes of my mouth weren't functioning. Bread had just started to have a smell for me again. During my illness it had tasted like clay, and I gave my ration to others. No, I am not pleading extenuating circumstances. I understood the baseness of my act the minute I enjoyed its reward. I felt unspeakably mean and wretched. So is it the bread you have banished me for, you who all stare ahead? Somebody could at least look my way. Those of you at least who used to rummage through the garbage heap for potato peels. Or who fought for the right to scrape the bottom of the kettle after noon rations were ladled out. Listen to me: you all know what I did later, when I worked as an interpreter... But it's true, I wasn't hungry when I worked as an interpreter. Being generous when you're not starving is no great achievement. I concede that. On the other hand, you can't help others if you don't conserve your own strength. It doesn't work any other way. I know what you're going to say. That all we medics, and anyone else who worked in the sick blocks, lived off the bread of corpses. When the stretchers carried the corpses to the storehouse, their squares of bread stayed on our table. Yes, we ate them. I know what you're thinking. That the crime wasn't in eating them but in counting on eating them. We knew exactly whose bread would stay. We weren't constantly, unremittingly hungry anymore, we medics, and we would become so involved in our work that at rations time we didn't focus all of our senses on the food. We didn't receive your bread like the faithful at Communion. We didn't contemplate the significance of your sacrifice. And after we stood naked, for what seemed like an eternity, in the cold dark night, and then greedily absorbed the shower's hot streams, we didn't ask what fuel was used to heat the water. We only wanted the warmth to last, and to be allowed to forget for a while the icy mountain air that would soon grip our naked bodies again. Like the tiles on the floor, we had been installed in this system. We ate your bread unceremoniously, like gravediggers putting away the dinner they've earned with their work. We grew accustomed. Man grows accustomed to everything. And apathetic. But you are right to judge me for the bread I received in exchange for cigarettes. I hadn't yet acquired the automatic movements of apathy. I could still feel the gnawing of hungry fox teeth in my stomach, and I knew exactly when I was crossing the line into the realm of base instinct. Yes, condemn me for that piece of bread. Because when the smoker's body finally succumbed, it succumbed in part because of the piece of bread I ate. If I had given him the cigarettes and not taken that one piece of bread, I would not have contributed to his death. Yes, I whispered, you are right to keep silent.

I began moving slowly, carefully down the steps, my tread noiseless because I was wearing sandals and not wooden clogs. It occurred to me that the formations along the terraces hadn't ignored me intentionally but that they simply could not see a living being with their weightless eyes. But, then, I shouldn't have been able to see them. I knew I was dreaming, yet beyond dreaming. As in camp, I slept, knowing that I slept. The next instant, the door to the washroom flew open and a herd of scrubbed and shaven-headed bodies poured out. Some ran toward the steps and began to scurry up, clutching their shirts and trousers, and the night shadows chased each other over their angular faces. The abrupt, resonant sound of clogs echoed off the steps. No one paid attention to me, so I looked elsewhere. I waited for the chimney up above to ignite into a huge red poppy. But the chimney was black, extinguished. You could see it faintly swaying, because at its base a flock of children had grabbed the steel cable that held it in place, and they were tugging with their little hands as if to topple it. Then the washroom door flew open again, and out came bodies whose bones formed horizontal figure-eights in their sides, and who had what looked like three small, shriveled nuts pressed into their crotches. One of the little girls covered her eyes, but the others stared as if they were seeing endless copies of a broken Pinocchio. Then all the children opened their eyes wide, very wide.

Translated by Michael Biggins.

Excerpts from
Memories of Yugoslavia

Drago Jančar

When life together in a marriage becomes unbearable, married partners decide upon divorce. And when, after long and tortuous discussions, terrible and universally degrading formalities, this finally occurs, an emptiness yawns upon both sides. The emptiness of the empty flat, the emptiness of life's amputation, the empty resonance of the quietness of what is missing, even though this may have been full of misunderstandings, yes, hatred even. But where there is hatred there is love, as every popular novel will tell us.

Reflection upon the urgent and unavoidable moment of the split between Slovenia and Yugoslavia fills me with unease. The tortuous discussions continue, the greedy partners are already stashing their wealth safely away, newspapers are already full of arguments as to how much this or that partner bought, acquired, and what each will pay to the other before they split. Reason argues that it must be so, for this country was never well established. And yet: we have lived our lives with it, by it, in it. I love Dalmatia, sentimental memories bind me to its wine nights, full of Mediterranean scents, the cool stones of her squares and churches. Antiquity, the Renaissance, the stillness in the gardens of the Catholic monasteries of the islands. Bosnian rivers, Sarajevo's unique blend of culture and religion, the bustle of oriental marketing, the fine, tiny hammers beating upon copper in the narrow streets. Biblical Macedonia, the bubbling speech of my Macedonian friends, full of feelings and witty turns of thought. The Danube, Novi Sad, where we celebrated transitory moments of theatrical glory during the theater festival, drowning the equally transitory moments of defeat. Belgrade, with its own perpetual vitality, its own morning scents from countless bakeries. Serbian colleagues with their black political humor, today apparently defeated, with their once refined irony and self-deprecation. Southern Serbia, Vranje, where, against my will, I spent a whole year of my life as a soldier, experiencing not only the loathsome barracks but also the paradoxical mixture of oriental sybaritism and Orthodox mysticism; the sweet sorrows of the Morava, the Slavic song accompanied by oriental drums. And finally Zagreb, even in this article loath to appearing on the same page as Belgrade or—God forbid—Southern Serbia. Zagreb with its eyes turned toward Vienna and both feet in the Balkans; Zagreb which is almost Slovenia but is still something else: its historical pathos, the Croat chessboard, the narrow Catholic mission, the center of the region that defends western civilization: *antemurale christianitatis*. Yes, Zagreb too will be in another country, to be known as the Republic of Croatia. And not without a touch of fearful egoism do I think about my own books on the shelves of booksellers in all those towns, in different languages, alphabets and dust jackets, and the stages of larger and smaller theaters where, with an intensity of mind and body, actors completed my fabrications.

Is all this really lost?

And I reflect again with unease upon the moment when I shall find myself exclusively among my beloved Slovenes, entering Europe, blabbing European phrases amid coarse industrialists and gentle singers, among kindred omniscience and its appropriate sarcasm, envy and malice. Before us lie solely pure aims and solutions. And "pure" solutions do not exist in my habitus. The hope remains that the new independent Slovenia will be a synthesis. First, a synthesis of what it already possesses, what the land inherited from a millennium of existence in the Central European space. This does not necessarily mean merely a sense of practicality and industriousness, but also its openness, curiosity and patience with differences within oneself and everything around. This means not only an eternal interest in one's own originality or a renewal of interest in one's Central European cultural neighbors, the Austrians, Czechs, Hungarians and Italians, but also in all creative, cultural human impulses, including those that will come from the former Yugoslavia.

But how we will manage and what we shall do with ourselves alone is another question. Only the future itself will actually answer all the mass of writing about the possibilities and requirements of independent Slovenian life. One thing is certain: No longer will anyone be able to argue that someone else is to blame for our lack of success, or that some unpleasant qualities in the Slovenian character are the consequence of ceaseless suppression, or that the organism cannot completely vitalize the economy or society develop completely because someone else is inhibiting this—once Vienna, then Rome, thirdly Belgrade, fourthly Moscow. No longer will Central European depression and a tendency to suicide be ascribable to external servitude.

Their Hearts Flamed for Yugoslavia

I probably do not speak solely for myself if I say that I love Yugoslavia, that is, the geography, the culture, the people. Yugoslav-ness—in other words, the Yugoslav idea—is something I hate from the bottom of my heart. Even more: I am sure that it is precisely the so-called Yugoslav-ers, the zealots of the idea of Yugoslavia, who have definitively destroyed Yugoslavia. The idea has stamped out the reality. Political terminology between the two wars accurately defined the notion of nationalism. The nationalists were Yugoslavs. They had their own organization known as ORYUN (Organization of Yugoslav Nationalists). Culturally this organization desired the unification of the Yugoslav nations, the removal of every difference, including linguistic ones. Socially they were narrow, loyal monarchists, devotees of the iron fist and the dictatorship that eventually came about. Left-wingers and cultural autonomists considered the black-uniformed armed guard who beat up and killed their political opponents throughout Slovenia and Dalmatia as fascists, which indeed they were. And yet they too were idealists. Their hearts flamed for a Yugoslavia united and indivisible, born of the fire and blood of the First World War. The idealism of the Yugoslav idea of this extreme right, in one differentiated form or another, reached far into many a head, including intellectual ones, from Serbian Piedmontists through Croat integralists to the Slovenian men of culture who had hated the defunct Austria, the "prison of nations." The Yugoslav idea found its most secure haven and dwelling-place within the army, "one of the best in Europe," as the newspapers of the time reported from maneuver to maneuver. Nevertheless, the army too collapsed at the first thrust in 1941.

Anyway, the Yugo-nationalism and integralism that forcibly and artificially concealed the actual state of affairs automatically triggered their own opposition: the collapse of Yugoslavia. A State of Croatia, supported by Berlin and Rome, came into existence, with limitless hostility toward Serbs, the East, everything that was not Croatian, European, western. They were undisturbed by the fact that Bosnian Muslims were accepted into their embrace, for according to their theories they were merely Croats of another faith. The Serbs organized their own units and the terrible massacre began, to be remembered throughout history as a dark, Balkan frenzy of bloody violence against everyone and everything. The Slovenes, the third nation of the happy triumvirate of SCS from 1918 were not mixed up in this battle. They were killing each other left and right, red and black. Let us leave the historical excursus, so confused and complicated as to have even today not arrived at any relevant historiography, and let us come to a halt with a summary: in 1941 Yugoslavia seemed lost forever. Neither former Yugoslavs—now again simply Croats, Serbs and Slovenes—believed in it any more, nor did those creating new maps of Europe, reflecting as they were upon the restoration of a Serbian state on the one hand and a beyond-the-Danube Central European federation on the other. At that time, those seizing upon and renewing the Yugoslav idea were those who a decade before had desired the destruction of this artificial Versailles creation and an independent Russian republic upon its soil. Such a plan for Slovenia was signed, in some document or other, by the communist parties of Italy and Austria. We shall never know whether the idea for the restoration of Yugoslavia grew in some Comintern Moscow office or in the heads of some suddenly integral Yugoslav thinking communists.

AN ERA OF IMMORTALITY

1945 saw Congress Square in Ljubljana witness again a glad throng. In 1945 Yugoslavia was renewed, born of blood, as they taught those of us who came into the world later, in our school lessons. An era of perpetuity and immortality had begun.

Not only did those of us who wore the Pioneer scarves about our necks, clenching infant fists in greeting to the immortally wonderful man in the white uniform, but also those who taught us all this, and the workers and soldiers as well—the whole of Yugoslavia believed itself to be living in an age that would never pass. No one gave any thought at all to the fact that the physical body of the man whose biography and the many songs about whom we all knew by heart would someday simply die. Once again the Yugoslav idea became exchanged for one of geography and culture. The intangible and immortal idea possessed an abstract triumvirate image: Tito-Yugoslavia-Communism. Of course, many thinkers produced entire subsystems of this triumvirate, with infinite numbers of analogies and variations that reached into every cell of the body of society. After the quarrel with Stalin, the Idea, in a sophisticated kind of way, was externally strengthened. Not merely politically and militarily. Jean Cassou and many others wrote eulogies to it. For the nations of Eastern Europe it signified hope. The Yugoslav rivers, the Adriatic Sea, the Alpine summits—none of this had any connection with reality anymore. All of these were merely metaphors for the idea of the trinity with its own subsystem. At the time, no one considered that—amid the magnificent dynamics of History—there were also the humiliated and sorrowful, the imprisoned, the tortured and the numerous killed. Not only was the price paid for the idea of Yugoslavia and its personification a high one during the war, but also after it. Fifteen thousand corpses were flung into Karst caves in the dark forests of Slovenia, and opponents were sentenced without trial at a time when peace had settled over the rest of the world. As the world sang of Tito's courage in confronting Stalin, one of the worst concentration camps of recent European history was opened on the Adriatic island of Goli. Zealots of the triune Yugoslav idea infiltrated the army, the secret police, factories and universities. And Yugoslavia, which really was more liberal than the remainder of Eastern Europe, became—as its dissident faction—the spoiled child of the West that was required to forgive the country's shadier deeds, for they were negligible when compared to the benefits and hopes otherwise aroused. And it must be said that in this Yugoslavia, too, life was not too hard to live. Needless to say, there was one condition: one must not even think anything against the triune deity and, increasingly, not even against the entire subsystem. To be a Croat, let us say, was to be quisling, a traitor, without a job or in prison. Farmer or Catholic—dangerous categories; an intellectual, if not a true Marxist, was suspect. And so on, down to the details described in numerous contemporary publications of already repetitive books of memoirs.

Yes, we lived through an era of immortality and perpetuity. One pop group achieved enormous popularity with a song entitled "The Name of Perpetuity," along the lines of "...and if perpetuity exists /and if perpetuity has a name / then that name is Tito's." "Yugoslavia, that's Tito," said the banners. And see, after his death, suggestions were indeed made, and indeed seriously discussed, about renaming Yugoslavia after him. I have no idea what—probably Titoslavia. I will not say Titoland, it would be as tasteless as all the general expectoration upon the dead president is becoming, against which not even the Committee for the Protection of the Person and Name of Marshal Tito, still in existence, can afford protection. Nowadays it seems to me that most of all I would myself like to afford him protection. Many of those now competing in the mudslinging are those who only yesterday elevated him to the heavens. A short while ago a Serbian writer exceeded everything, speaking in holy wrath and suggesting that Josip Broz be exhumed from his grave, to be impaled upon a branch of hawthorn.

Fresh zealots are again at work. If I am here concerned about anything linked with Tito, it is this unfortunate idea of Yugoslav-ness that has elevated itself above reality, to bury the latter beneath itself.

In truth many a man in the street considers that things were all right under Tito, better than today anyway. As those who were citizens under Emperor Franz Joseph and are still living today can tell us, bread was cheaper then.

A 99.9% COMMUNIST ARMY

Matters in Yugoslavia went well only as long as they were going well in comparison to something else. This something else was the remainder of Eastern Europe, which was continuously worse off. So it was that Yugoslavs looked upon Romanians, Poles, even Czechs and Hungarians with a mixture of pride, derision and pity—sentiments springing from the link with the Orient. There was some solidarity but only a little, very little. Self-satisfaction prevailed. Some skeptics, particularly in the western regions of the country, where daily comparisons with life in Italy and Austria were possible, were even then vociferously drawing attention to the relativity of the self-satisfaction of the Yugoslavs. The veils upon the Marshal's life began to drop; inflation, the signs of an even greater recession, unemployment, workers moving from the south of the country to the north, from the country into Western Europe. According to the criteria prevailing at the time, these migrations were in the main a sign of the right to free movement and employment. And it was true, but this apparent liberty concealed a whole wave of fears and repressions within the State, also concealing the latent state of crisis in the country's economy, to be increasingly rapidly revealed.

After the death of the Marshal it was soon evident with what means the relative social peace and aforementioned self-satisfaction of the citizens had been purchased: a vast mountain of dollar debts, so large it was impossible to see beyond.

After the disintegration of part of the Soviet empire, after the establishment of democracy, first in Hungary and then elsewhere, the painful truth revealed itself to even those final few who, right up to that very moment, had thought that Yugoslavia was the enshrinement of Tito, from whose route we were never going to diverge, the waving of flags after basketball matches and empty blustering in every sphere of life. By then even they were forced to admit the truth, all of them, the cunning and the naive, for it penetrated at least to their brains if not to their credulous hearts, when they began to ask about their own empty pockets: rampant inflation gone wild, an economy falling apart. The quasi-reforms and fresh debts those in authority brought from the West as reckoning for their own former, counter-Soviet position provided no relief. And none of yesterday's methods can assist any more: complete economic ruin, vast unemployment, the explosion of social conflicts which in this country will also become national ones—all this lies at our door.

I do not know how Tito succeeded in "leading the thirsty across the water"—this very expression used in praise of his cunning and in mockery of his victims, how he used Western politics and his anti-Soviet flexibility to squeeze out of them fresh and fresher support and loans. In reality the whole country, and above all the army, was saturated with communist ideals and values. Every adult Yugoslav male who has been in the army knows that he existed for that year in a fortress of the most orthodox, most backward, most dogmatic communism. And is it this army that would be the ally of the West in any crisis? Who on earth believed that? No one in Yugoslavia. Apparently everyone in the West.

Today, Western politicians and strategists can still be found who see in this still 99.9% communist army some kind of surety for some kind of stability in this part of the world. With their mathematical and geopolitical and strategic studies, those pragmatists who turned their backs upon principles have done more harm to mankind than the principalists who are not innocent either. Did not the West shower bloody Ceaucescu with aid merely because he directed a somewhat, fractionally better, independent foreign policy?

Needless to say, it was not the Western strategists who paid for this; these politics were paid for in blood by the Romanians. And they are still paying today.

If, upon the death of Tito, upon the wailing of the sirens and scenes of ancient sorrow, we knew that some epoch was drawing to its certain close, that the immortal and infinite is also mortal and finite, then we saw the final collapse of the greatest eschatological idea of this century during the Christmas days of 1989. Television, that crazy anti-Gutenburg invention, made it impossible to read dramatic literary scenes about this. Live and direct, day after day, hour after hour, we were shown the drama of the bloody king who today strode down the red carpet at the airport, the next day was having his blood pressure measured in some back-of-beyond military corner just before being shot to death. And the tyrant's kingdom in chaos and blood.

And only here did an era truly end, in the manner in which it had begun. I am terribly afraid that final scenes, which also have wonderful moments—the bringing down of walls, the embracing, the dissident writer raised more or less from prison to throne—are also followed by epilogues. In the Soviet Union, in Yugoslavia. In both countries where the nature of the world has not only been forced in the social sense, but where they have also attempted to alter the country's organic, that is, its cultural image. In the Soviet Union theoreticians and practitioners have created the so-called Soviet; in SFRJ, the Yugoslav nation. And brought up a whole mass of people who also believe in these constructions. For some, fiction has become reality, but wakened reality cannot acknowledge it as such.

This Matter Could Not End Well

The final illusion that the Yugoslav, that is the socialist, that is Tito's idea, in relation to world communist eschatology, is in actual fact a Protestant one, came to us at the end of the seventies. Reforms brought a liberal atmosphere, and those of us who were of an age when the young person is being formed took this condition to be self-evident. We were unaware that this idea did in fact pulsate within its universal, fraternal, ideological arena. We did not believe that the Yugoslav "protestants" had once before double-crossed the Hungarians, and we believed even less that they would abandon the Czechs who had borne our Communist Luther upon their shoulders through Prague. Not one of us even imagined that the Cold Fifties might return to us. Consequently, we all, alone and together, paid for our liberalism, left-wing notions and nationalism. The seventies arrived, Czech quislings embraced our leaders at airports. Tito returned from a visit to Kim Il Sung, and hordes of joyous people repeated the scenes from Korea, week after week in Europe, scattering flowers along the roads he drove along. I do not know whether he was interested in anything else at the time, but the zealots took matters into their own hands, to the very end. His portrait became as sacred as in the fifties, then on account of the "revolution that still continues," now because of inertia and the fervor of zealots. There was not even any room for Schweik-like jokes. Flies were not allowed to defecate on these portraits. My naive friend, who like many had joined the Party after the occupation of Czechoslovakia (many fell for the unusually paradoxical campaign of those years, against all logic and reason) once came to see me in despair. His daughter had returned from kindergarten to clearly tell her parents: I love you both, but not as much as Comrade Tito. To love Comrade Tito, to proclaim yourself a Yugoslav (never a Slovenian, a Croat or even an individual) became more than a matter of patriotism. This was a matter of ideology.

Yugoslavia at the end of the sixties—acknowledging her own differences, cultural peculiarities, diverse thoughts on life and the world—drew near to something of a contract with reality. During the seventies, the country again became only the triune Idea. But because the country had open boundaries (proof of its self-confidence and great belief in itself), the work of the zealots grew more and more difficult. Reality did exist elsewhere. The zealots threw themselves into the fight with truth with ever greater patriotic fire: flags, stadium rituals, pop songs, the subtle declarations by the literati, the chant of Yu-go-sla-vi-a or Ti-to-Ti-to brought tears of emotion back to the eyes of many. Those of us observing this fresh wave of delirium from the wings or behind bars—and there were more than a few of us there during the seventies—knew then that this matter could not end well.

A BALKAN INN

During those few years when the country was known as the Kingdom of Serbs, Croats and Slovenes, prior to the start of the dictatorship that was to rename itself Yugoslavia in 1929, matters, at least at first glance, did appear to be in order. The militant Serbian, cultural Croatian, and economically successful Slovenian peoples, each of them with its own piece of the power and the glory. And even here, with these sample indications of the Yugoslav idyll, we encounter dual difficulties. The first is a stereotype, well enough expressed by the Croatian writer Miroslav Krleža: God spare us from the

Serbian cannon and Croatian culture. The second is linked to reality. Also living here are Macedonians, considered to be southern Serbs, Muslims who were thought of as Turkified Serbs and Croats, and Albanians, considered to be Arnauts, in other words, only worthy of Karl May and his novel *In the Land of the Shiptars*. Even as early as this, Slovenes were convinced that they were being taken advantage of economically and subjected to cultural unification. The Croats believed that they were suppressed, the Serbs that they did not possess the leading role their military victories deserved. Hence in the new socialist state the communists took particular care not to repeat the issue that had divided the first Yugoslavia, using their own theoretical aims in the form of Lenin's theory on the question of nationality. When establishing the republics, they granted the Albanians an autonomous region within the province of Serbia. Needless to say these "republics" did not possess any authority; everything was controlled from the center, the Politburo. The greater the rights of the republic (and the individual) as written in the laws that were altered every few years amid great pomp, the lesser their actual possibility. As we said, the Idea was Yugoslavization, and the most numerous nation, the Serbs, were the people who seized upon it most avidly. This concept was also introduced as a nationality category into the population census. Forty years later and after an incredible amount of energy had been invested in this new people, only one million Yugoslavs could be counted among the twenty million inhabitants of the country. After Tito's death, the rapidly cracking cement of "Yugoslav-ness" soon revealed what lay below.

A memory returns: it was 1979. We were seated in the marvelous Roman arena in Pula, at the annual open-air, beneath-the-stars Yugoslav film festival that presents the latest films from the whole country. For long years these had been of the variety where the audience enthused wildly if one partisan was shot and twenty Germans fell, and sighed sadly when twenty Germans were shot and one partisan fell. That evening we were waiting for a different kind of film; we had already seen an extraordinary introductory film. A documentary from Kosovo was shown. A portrait of the life of a large Albanian family, several generations beneath one roof, each family with its own hearth. Halfway through the film was its conclusion—every member of the family coming down the steps of the house, one after the other, from the youngest to the oldest. The message was clear: we are here. You may reckon us Arnauts or the Shiptars of Karl May, you can say we have spread into ancient Serbian regions, but we are here and no one can alter that fact. The Serbs, with their ancient cultural monuments, monasteries, the cradle of the medieval land of Serbia in Kosovo itself, could not bring themselves to acknowledge this, as the bearers and supporters of the Yugoslav idea could not accept the truth that, in fact, the Yugoslav nation does not exist. The first eruptions in Kosovo came two years later—demonstrations with the demand for an independent republic. These demonstrations were suppressed by force, as have been all the others since.

In the years following, it was rapidly made clear that not only were the Albanians in this country dissatisfied, but everyone, all the peoples, including national minorities. As if Lenin's principles had solved nothing in any field whatsoever, although these solutions had been endlessly praised. By the mid-eighties it was obvious—if we summarize very briefly and not without some fear of stereotypes—that the Slovenes were dissatisfied because they were being made use of economically and were culturally under threat; similar reasons applied to the Croats, and additionally because Serbs had been put in power at every level in their own republic of Croatia, from the secret police to the government. The Serbs registered discontent because they had lost their own sovereignty in Yugoslavia and the Albanians in Kosovo were repressing them, destroying their ancient culture, while the developed North (Slovenia and Croatia), as was generally known, was taking advantage of the underdeveloped South and not the other way around. The Macedonians were economically bankrupt, and Yugoslavia was not doing anything at all toward their international recognition. The Albanians were discontented because they were suffering universal repression from the Serbian police and the army. Similar reasons for discontent in Yugoslavia existed for the Montenegrins, Muslims, the Hungarians in Vojvodina, the Italians in Istria. Stereotypes grow rapidly: the Slovenes are Austro-types and separatists, hate the army and are undermining the State; the Croats are a genocidal nation, rotten rebels, supporters of the Vatican-Comintern connection; the Macedonians are parasites; the Montenegrins lazy sods; the Albanians primitives and rapists; the Muslims are Khomeini's men.

Chaos. Who is able to understand it? The aforementioned Krleža described this condition as similar to a Balkan inn, all of those within already somewhat drunk and dangerous. And all of them waiting, waiting for when one of them smashes the light. This metaphor has been accepted into the phraseology of daily talk in Yugoslavia.

"THE ISLAND OF FREEDOM" AND IRRATIONALISM

Last year the fracturing of Communism throughout Eastern Europe rendered the Yugoslav picture a little clearer. Diverse opinions, and not merely those of the Politburo, but also writers' and philosophers' phantasmagoria on the state of the country and society, were laid aside. Finally we were united in the desire to show through elections what the truth was. The elections in Slovenia, the first republic to hold them, gave the communists approximately the same percentage as in Czechoslovakia. In Croatia they suffered total defeat; in Serbia, renamed Socialists, they achieved an absolute majority. In Montenegro, now under a completely Serbian leadership, they won under the good old name of communist. In Bosnia and Hercegovina the voters divided their votes among the national parties: Muslim, Serbian and Croatian. The Albanians boycotted the Serbian elections, Macedonia remained divided among the nationalists, the Yugoslav reformists and the communists.

In short, the East remained Red, as in Romania and Bulgaria. I am not interpreting that maliciously but am merely noting that the cultural ingredients are older and more powerful than the ideas they wish to enforce. Nor do I write with malice because our Serbian colleagues endlessly drone on at us about the democratic traditions of their own nation and the provincial Central European-ness of the Croats and Slovenes. I note this with sorrow. During the difficult seventies, when the atmosphere in Belgrade was more liberal than that of Slovenia, it was our Serbian colleagues who assisted us a great deal. Numerous links were forged then, and later in the eighties when, in the Slovenia that *Newsweek* described as "an island of freedom," we were publishing prohibited and persecuted Serbian authors. I write with sorrow because I feel that it is not communism that has won among the Serbs but rather irrationalism, the Kosovo "convulsion."

And it is indeed writers who have contributed to this, the Serbs' holy war against the Albanians and anyone attempting to understand them. The passions that have come to light, the gigantic potential of a traditionally politicized Serbian nation, have been used by the professionals for the irrational, for ideas far from reality: the rule of communists. The result is that only half of Yugoslavia still has communists in power, still blinding themselves and others with the "Yugoslav" idea, while the other half has two democratic states, Croatia and Slovenia, that no longer want any dealings with irrationalism of the Balkan and communist kind.

THE "SARDINE-TUNNEL" AND A LYRICAL THEME

The story of writers in the East who found themselves involved in politics whether they wished to be or not is well known and needs no repetition. Those who overnight moved from prison and silence to some leading position ceaselessly in the limelight will soon realize that intelligence, an ethical stance and enlightened reasoning are not only insufficient for political pragmatism but also even sometimes undesirable. Many a bitter disappointment awaits them, not least the realization—never foreign to them but evidently always only applicable to others—that the world of politics, power and authority is indeed something different from the world of literature. But what awaits those of our colleagues who have lost all sense of self-reflection, who are dragging their readers or their own people who blindly trust them, into a dangerous sphere, into violence?

Did we, I ask myself, talk for so many years about politics not interfering in literature, only for some *literati* to now be interfering in politics in a more obscure manner than the politicians themselves?

Some years ago, when the constricting band around Yugoslavia began to break, the first signs of national impatience began to appear. Nothing untoward for anyone in any way cognizant of the soul of this terminally ill country. The violence in Kosovo—unfortunately elevated by some of our colleagues into a sacred creed in order to defend the justifiable matter of eternal Serbian-ness—has cooled the traditionally good relationships between Slovenes and Serbs. In Slovenian and Serbian P.E.N. we agreed on open panel discussions, which we held in public in both Ljubljana and Belgrade. We failed to agree upon nearly everything. Our support for democracy in Slovenia was to them "particularist,"our tales of Central Europe "provincial." Their Kosovo traumas were to us "anachronistic," their submission to Milošević's charisma, which was to legally turn the Serbian question into a post-Tito, post-Comintern Yugoslavia, was to us submission to a national Bolshevism. Of course, I am simplifying matters, the talks were far more complicated and wittier than can be conveyed here. Nevertheless, we did talk. Now we no longer even talk. The last chat I had with a Serbian colleague, a fighter for the sacred matter of the Serbian people and their Orthodox tradition, was after a fresh wave of violence in Kosovo, when the police drove young Albanians through the so-called "sardine-tunnel," beating them up as they passed through. I expressed not only my personal protest but also the fear that this madness would spread throughout the whole of Yugoslavia, which has bitter, the bitterest, experience of national quarrels. Western Europe, itself far from innocent in this sense, came to its senses after the last war. Here in Yugoslavia, where so much blood has been spilled, everything indicates that we are prepared to repeat it all over again. Is it not time for us at least to keep quiet if we are not even now capable of raising a voice against everything that is being prepared? Perhaps I was somewhat pathetic, but he was even more cynical. "What you are saying," he said, "is nothing but a lyrical theme." If this writer, Miodrag Bulatović, the Serbian expert on the lyrical theme, and I could not agree upon even the care for human life and its dignity, then I really do not know what else we have left to discuss. Of course, someone can always be found to state that something greater than life does exist: the truth. The Serbian truth, the Albanian truth. Between them are knives and an epic theme. Always anew. Let me be allowed to step aside from this debate. Let me be allowed to take an interest in something else in this world.

We Up Here, You Down There

Our deceased president liked to make use of the phrase, "We up here, you down there." This meant that they up there with all the responsibility arranged something that we down here were to implement with all responsibility. I was the editor of a student newspaper, and such a haranguing of the people seemed unprecedented to me. We published a cartoon depicting two granite blocks. Carved on the upper one was "we up here," and on the lower, "you down there." The upper one cracked, fell apart. This cartoon caused us grave trouble with the zealots of Communism. But it was not that. It was that people accepted this as something natural. Now, when writer colleagues also speak of major and minor cultures of peoples, of the ancient and more recent peoples of Yugoslavia, of statesmen or bondsmen, even of lower races (Albanians), I understand why that syntagma was so ingenuously received. In the Balkans there is always someone up above and someone down below. As in Byzantium. Or the Ottoman empire. Rulers above, the small fry below. One nation above, another below. The bureaucratic Party caste above, the kulaks and reactionaries below. One violent, the other fearful. The ones above, whenever they are in power, must make use of that power, otherwise they are deemed worthless. If by any chance a Parliament convenes in which everyone wishes to be equal, Croatian delegates shoot themselves there. It sometimes looks as if the traumas of the recent and distant past have simply crept under the skin of the people here, entering their genetic structure. I have no other explanation for the state in which writers lend their brains and their pens to prove national, cultural and political superiority. And if this is so, no intelligent idea, no modern sociological or social method, no consequential democratic suggestion or system will save Yugoslavia.

In a land where every thought is shaped with regard to "up here" or "down there," every idea will also be altered into a political pragmatism. In such a land the subtlety of the soul will always be subjugated to the kings, heroes, drums and gods; it will be impossible to hide from them. As through all the years to date, history will continue to knock once at every home in one uniform or another. Those "down there," circumspect in the face of whatever authority, will continue to ask, as does the peasant in Euripedes' *Electra*, "[W]hich man, which hero, which god? And who are those people?... What noise is that? Am I allowed to be what I have been? To knead bread, chop wood, desire my wife? Which man, which hero, which god?"

After free elections and after all the changes in Europe, political prisoners still abound in Yugoslavia. The January 1991 issue of *The Index on Censorship*, published in London,is enough. Three columns of data close to home, all from Serbia, the majority from the unhappy region of Kosovo, three columns of data behind which lie the human stories of imprisonment and repression. And where are the thousands of tales from the "tunnel of sardines" and from earlier years throughout the whole country? Rendered as it is through the principle of "up here, down there" it is impossible to avoid history here, even by fleeing into the streets.

AND NOW, DEAR GOD, WITH TEETH BARED

Yugoslavia is a chaotic part of the European world. To me it also seems ungovernable. And it also seems to me, and possibly I exaggerate, that because a metaphor for the deeper chaos of the world can be sensed here, all are washing their hands of it. This conglomeration of cultures, civilizations and religions, Byzantine, Catholic and European rationalistic ingredients, reflects the confusion of the world, where reason—linear and arranging-the-world—shrugs its shoulders with the argument: I do not understand.

Even if television were not serving us half-hourly snippets of a condensed, chaotic image of the world every evening, even if the world about us and around us, the world of Yugoslav shouting today, the forerunner of tomorrow's madness and pains, were not definitively chaotic: the fact would always remain that, in his dealings with and even in his ideas about the world from earth to heaven, twentieth century man is no longer capable of control. It does seem as if today all man's endeavors, from let us say the spiritual, the ethical through technology, science and economics, are directed toward making life more bearable, more tolerant, greater in material comfort and more controllable from every aspect. In actual fact, outbreaks of impatience of the most different kinds are growing increasingly worse, even those we thought belonged to the previous century. Man simply no longer has any check over what is happening in the world or within himself. Communists and Nazis have compromised all the enlightened mottoes of earlier centuries, and instead of orderly social and national states we now have a murderous weld that has intensified the worst that existed in individual and national collective ideas. How can I understand Yugoslavia, how can I carry on being mixed up in the ordering of affairs when the world as such is not in order? Hordes of one kind or another have been rolling across the European cultural continent for centuries, shouting slogans: religious, national, social. Some persons stride stiffly along red airport carpets: salvoes, national anthems, secretive and unclear reports from behind closed doors, reports followed by boycotts, economic wars, assassinations, real wars. Nor have all-redeeming economy and technology redeemed anything. Some sniper shoots twenty people from a tenth floor. Some Korean rushes around Seoul from morning until night on behalf of his computer business and to buy a new car, instead of seating himself beneath a tree to reflect upon the harmony of the principle of male and female, as he did two decades ago. What I want to say is that there is more to our lives than the bare history of logical causes and effects. As in the world at large, there is also a great deal that is irrational in the Yugoslav confusion. I know that this interpretation will not be of any assistance to anyone, least of all in the example given.

Nevertheless it can at least serve to illustrate the fact that people do exist who have had enough of risking their lives and reason, words and actions, so that some country called Yugoslavia can enter at least the twenty-first century as a democratic, modern and free country, a country without any political violence of any kind, without an unbearable self-perpetuating practice of threats and intimidation, a ceaseless "we up here, you down there."

I have already spent half my life pleading for the respect of difference, for the reciprocity of differences, national, cultural, individual, creative. And, ever anew, the result is always that at the end these differences stand opposite each other, with teeth bared. Ever since I encountered reason, in other words, skepticism, I have put up with all the Yugoslavist, communist symbolics, its iconography, its Marshal's stadium rituals, with the utmost diffi-culty. Beneath these worked the secret police, the courts, the military appa-ratus, fear in every cell of the micro-organisms of society. And now, dear God, when there's an end to it all: fresh potentates with coats of arms, mot-toes, fluttering flags, troops in formation already appearing to me. It is not the same, I do know that, but couldn't they have thought of something else? Something that would not ceaselessly, persistently remind us of the yester-day still squatting nightmarishly upon our chests?

TODAY LITHUANIA, TOMORROW SLOVENIA?

This has been a writer's prejudice. Truly, democracy in Slovenia is not working as one would hope. Parliament is squabbling over minutiae, the people peep askance at the new authorities through their fingers: vast amounts of malice, narrowness, constant anger. Today they have already forgotten yesterday, let alone what will happen tomorrow. All the same, even the worst democracy is better than none at all, and infinitely better than tanks on the streets. As I finish this article, tanks are at this very moment on the streets of Vilnius. Lithuania is experiencing the same fate as Czechoslovakia in 1968.

I had wanted to end this article at this point, drawing attention to the rel-ativity of man's freedom even in the national, democratic countries, to the relationships between the authorities and the individual, which are deeper than social legalities and from which we shall not be able to retreat with our own questions and criticisms, even in the newly emerging republic of Slovenia, achieved calmly through referendum.

Now I must finish it differently. The fate of Lithuania is also the fate of Slovenia. Europe, of which we in precisely Lithuania, Slovenia and other small eastern European countries talk so much, ought to know that this is also her fate.

The movement for the independence of Slovenia is actually an ancient matter. Only the one that ended in a referendum last December did not begin with nationalism. It began with the fight for man's rights, with the writing of literary magazines, courageous columnists, with alternative movements, with the persistent, calm resistance of the Slovenian Catholics. It began with the movement for the freedom of the individual, for democ-racy, for pluralism. And Slovenia—in other words, the many thinking and politically active people in the land—has long thought that it would be pos-sible to achieve this through a change in circumstances within Yugoslavia.

The Yugoslav army, the prime defender of Yugoslav and careful guardian of communist ideas, responded by imprisoning three young journalists and one sublieutenant from its own ranks. And only then was Congress Square once again filled to overflowing. Fifty thousand people demanded their release, and since 1988, when this occurred, right until today, attempt after attempt has been made to alter conditions in Yugoslavia, one after the other doomed to fail. The arrogance of a people that has long lost touch with reality has been shown to be boundless. And it has been here that matters have matured into the decision to render valid the right to self-determination. Slovenia co-founded this country of Yugoslavia. If, after seventy years of long reflection, the great majority of its citizens no longer wish to live in it, then this unit also has the right to leave. I do not know when European diplomacy will accept the fact that this decision is irrevocable. I do not know when the European public will begin to deal with the problems relevant to its own continent and rather less with those of South American coups. It does not appear that this will be soon; it does seem as if with the disappearance of the German Democratic Republic from the European map the last great problem is thought to have been solved.

I am afraid it will have to be unhappy Lithuania that will prove this is not so. And tomorrow Slovenia? Croatia? Kosovo? The whole of Yugoslavia?

Last week someone high up in the European world lectured in Ljubljana. He was greatly in favor of youthful Slovenian democracy, and his audience was grateful for his goodwill. With satisfaction he ascertained that pluralism and respect for man's rights have now, thanks to the World, spread to eastern Europe. When he had finished, some ignorant listener raised his hand to ask whether the right to self-determination of nations belongs to the fundamental Rights of Man, that ancient principle Slovenia had called upon in 1918. Absolutely, he replied, but for Slovenia, that very moment carrying out its referendum, of great value, there were some legal reservations; it was not a sovereign state. But what must Slovenia or Lithuania do to become this, when in 1918 a referendum answer would have sufficed? They must take over all authority upon their own territory, came the answer, they must become sovereign. And what if Russian tanks roll into Lithuania tomorrow or the tanks of the Yugoslav army appear on the streets of Ljubljana? You will have every moral support, replied the dignitary. Thank you, replied the naive listener, the writer of these lines.

Translated by Anne Čeh.

The Summer Battle

Ivo Štandeker

I was going to write a war report, but all that remained in my mind were
the dead and the wounded.

The truck drivers at the third roadblock between Maribor and Šentilj,
mustached and sweaty with waiting, already trapped a whole day between
the two sides of a war they couldn't figure out. The Bulgarian had a ring, an
enormous gold ring shaped like an eagle, and wondered what good the ring
was to him now that he was going to die. "It's all gonna work out just fine,"
I told him. Ten minutes later he was dead. The chipper Turk trying to mask
his fear talked on and on about how this truck was hauling detergent and
that was alright, but those other two carried meat and that wasn't alright
because it would soon start to smell, and how it would be great if they were
finally allowed to go home. Soon he was lying amid the other bodies, his
white teeth still flashing through his bloody face. And then there was the
young Turk with light eyes who just stood there, not saying a word. Gone.
And the unfortunate man from Maribor, the only Slovenian among the lot,
who was so angry. "I'm not gonna say anything, don't take any pictures,"
as he squatted down by his truck. "Don't walk here, they'll shoot, I got nothing to do with politics." After, we stayed with the others long enough, facing the tanks with their engines running, and when they still didn't shoot,
he joined us at last. Dead.

And Frenk. Forgive me, Frenk, for not coming in the ambulance with you.
Sturdy Frenk, clean-shaven and cool. I first met him when the tanks reached

the second roadblock, the train on the track at Ranca. While a couple of reporters and locals hung around the last tank, making this or that remark to goad their confusion into courage, Frenk remained silent, his lips pressed into a smile. His truck had stayed three kilometers back, before Pesnica, at the first roadblock, which the tanks had just finished blasting away and squashing into a pulp. A mound of burning iron, rubber and beef, blending the molten metal and the asphalt underneath. But Frenk's not a whiner, he's the kind of man who simply starts over from scratch. So he just smiled and watched the tanks as they left the road and plowed their way through the fields to bypass the freight train put in their path. "They're gonna have trouble," was all he said. Then he showed us dirt roads in the hills which could be used to avoid the barricades, and we followed the tanks in a Renault 4. There was such indecision in their halting progress along the muddy snail-trail by the edge of the woods that we walked around them quite at our ease and took photos. Meanwhile, Frenk sketched the scene. He used to be on a tank crew himself, and he knew about things. How the engine of this one sounded like it was on its last leg, and about the exhaust fumes of that one, choked ventilators, they wouldn't last long. It was more than twenty-four hours now that the tanks had been on their barge-through-any-obstacle way, and they'd used up a lot of fuel, too much. Šentilj was going to be tough. The last border crossing. The most important one. The little valley of access was becoming increasingly narrow for tanks, and it led straight to the third and final pre-frontier roadblock at Štrihovec.

FIRST FIGHT. When the tanks came to a halt in front of the roadblock, Diego and I were already on this side of it. It was Friday, only nine goddamn a.m., and despite the forecast to the contrary, the day was turning sunny and fair. At Frangež's house, this side of the track and the roadblock, there was a pell-mell of territorial defense troops, reporters, and local inhabitants. We looked about for a vantage point and decided on the roof of the house. We found a ladder somewhere, put it up against the lean-to, climbed up, pulled up the ladder behind us, and leaned it against the roof. It was too damn high; we had to scale half of it on all fours before we were able to straddle the ridge. But the view from above was well worth the effort. Yonder, some ten tanks were waiting; opposite them, seven large trucks were lined up in one lane. Behind the trucks there was the track with the long freight train, and nearest the house three additional pairs of trucks. From the wooded slopes left and right of the house an occasional broken sentence floated up on the breeze, from where the territorial defense was stationed. Down below us was still all commotion, people asking us anxiously what was going on. "One tank's coming," Diego yelled back.

It came down the slope on the left side, behind the brook and the bush, slowly rolling in reconnaissance. The people below us darted from corner to corner to catch a glimpse of it, and behind a stack of firewood close to the house a territorial defender waited, clutching the bazooka slung over his shoulder. "We're not letting them through this roadblock without a fight," we'd been told earlier. One heart beat. So simple and simultaneous. A discharge, Diego takes a picture, the tank shudders, smoke. And nothing else, just the silence of the engine cut off. The turret hatch opened and below us people emerged. Confusion, real confusion was the thing which surprised us most. "They're giving up, don't shoot, don't shoot," we yelled from the roof. We took that last part for granted but were somewhat apprehensive nevertheless. "Hold your fire," one of our officers tried to be decisive. "They've got weapons," came another voice. "Kill 'em, kill the bastards," someone below us hollered, a civilian who spoke Serbo-Croatian all the time, we didn't know why. It felt as though everyone's fuse would blow any second, and the sun made our clothing stick to our sweaty skin.

"Don't shoot!" A reedy, breaking, very desperate voice. The first of the tank crew to surrender was a youth from Ljubljana. "Are you totally nuts?" he kept sobbing as he stumbled toward us. "Are you all out of your minds?" Two more surrendered, and we decided we'd better climb down, then another two surrendered, two were wounded, heat-shell burns. One of the wounded, a Macedonian, had lost an eye; the other one was from Zadar. There was no first aid. "We have something ready in Šentilj," someone said, but the soldiers had a first aid kit with some gauze, and Ma Frangež tried to wash and bandage the wounded. Neighbors in sandals rode over on scooters to help, TV cameras hummed, there was an awful lot of talk going on, questions were fired at the captured, nobody knew what was going on, nobody thought of offering them a cigarette. I gave them a Marlboro each, then I went in search of the man who seemed to be the highest ranking territorial defense officer in the group. The tanks on the other side were perfectly still, and I was filled with misgivings.

"Excuse me, are you in charge of this operation?"

"No, the regional headquarters is."

"But you have the highest rank here."

"Yes."

"Why don't you pull these civilians away, then, before someone gets hurt?"

"We'll let you know if it gets dangerous." He was so embarrassed he failed to realize his own agitation and absurdity. Diego and I were fed up with it all and cautiously crawled to the peace and quiet on the other side of the train.

SECOND FIGHT. You somehow figure that as long as you leave them alone they won't shoot at you, or at least, if they do, you won't get hit right away; that way you can get by. But the tanks were motionless, absolutely, totally motionless. In the shade beneath the trucks, there by the ditch, people sat on their haunches. Truck drivers from Turkey, Greece and Bulgaria, whose vehicles had been placed there a day earlier by our people, without the truckers having any say in the matter. Or possibility of retreat. They weren't happy about it, they told us. As none of us could think of anything to put matters right, we squatted next to them and kept them company. Until Diego grew restless and said he wanted to get back and we said goodbye and left. When we'd gotten to the other side of the train, the planes came.

The first round was a warning. A few truckers sprinted to safety. Everybody was running somewhere. Two planes came, then another two, Migs I think. In moments like that you have to keep your wits about you, but I didn't know how to just yet. When the second couple of planes were approaching, Diego and I had already reached the house, and then they did indeed open fire. A spray of bullets raced past us along the courtyard. The hallway. In the kitchen the grandma was wringing her hands. Another volley. All the windows were open because of the heat. Diego shouted that the bullets were ricocheting. From an old Grundig radio set on the fridge, President Kučan was making a speech. When the planes flew off in the opposite direction, it was safe to peek outside. The third onslaught. Diego is ready and takes photos. Then he hurls himself inside after me. Now we have a photo, now we're not budging any more. Explosions. "They're firing missiles."

"Does it kill you if it hits the house?"

"Depends." We breathe.

AFTERWARDS. When it was over it seemed there wasn't a soul anywhere. No moaning. Something had to be done. "What about the people by the trucks? We run around the far side of the garden, to be safer. Now the tanks might come. Smoke from behind the train, and a woman shouting in English for somebody to get the fucking stretchers over there, that they are mortally wounded. We slither under the cars. Another world. The trucks are demolished, glass, mud. Right up front a woman is dragging a body; the tanks beyond her are as yet motionless. We run. "Watch out, the truck's gonna blow," she shouts. Right, it's on fire, dangerously so. The ground's slippery, I fall. To keep away from the blast we cross a meadow. Water everywhere. In the ditch near the first truck lie the dead and the injured, who are terribly wounded, and what can we do. Back at the train two medics appear in white. "We have serious casualties here," I call out to them. "Watch out, the truck might explode. Come way around there." They can't make it. They turn around and run back. Diego and the woman, who must also be a photographer, are dragging bodies out of the ditch. I try to hold the upper body but it's heavy and it's difficult to get a grip. They're all out now. Some of them are dead, one's sitting up and groaning. There are at least three others alive. We need to call for help. The two of them stay there, I run back. It's so far. There's no time for the detour. Behind the wheels of a truck there's another one dead. The head. On the other side of the train there's no one. Near the house a territorial comes running toward me, alone. "Yes, I'm a medic." I tell him where to go. He seems OK. He starts off. He tells me to bring the stretchers, which are supposed to be over there some-where. I can't find them. Time's flying. I must find something, anything. I search around the buildings. The ladder, it'll do. It's hard to run with a lad-der. I push it over the link between two boxcars. Two ambulances drive up. "Quick, we need three stretchers over there."

"No way. It's too far. We'll have to drive around, over the hills."

"OK. We'll wait."

Back again. Over the train. Past the trucks. The medic has attended to them in the meantime, given them shots. Just one more wounded to go. Frenk.

Later, during a lull in the fighting, we went over the whole story a hun-dred times. Searching for reasons. Frenk had already left, but he had come back before the attack with the American photographer, Jana Schneider. They went to the Turks right after we'd left and she took pictures. After the air-raid she was the only one left unscathed. But Jana had just arrived from Ethiopia and this was her thirteenth war, while for Frenk it was his first. He lay there with his legs shot through and I don't know what in his chest, and he was conscious. Jana was holding his hand, my poor baby, and he was brave. "I wanna see my legs."

"It's OK, believe me." Diego held the lower leg, I held the thigh, the medic bandaged the area in between which was missing. I forgot his name, the medic's. He was good, calm. "Ever done this before?"

"No." We needed to keep them all in the shade. "They're gonna be here any minute now." One of the wounded died.

Then we just waited. And photographed every fucking detail to preserve it at least in the photos. And waited. The tanks were still there. With measured strides Mustachio approached. That's what I had named him in my mind before, when I first saw him. When the tanks had trundled over the meadows, he had walked in front. Solitary and tall, with a tank commander's cap, a full mustache on his tragically serious face, his back ramrod straight as if at permanent attention. A man who doesn't need a tank. Captain Zekič, I was told that evening by the soldiers. He was not in command of the unit, some moron with twigs on his helmet was, who kept prattling on about a CIA conspiracy. But Mustachio was the spirit of the unit. He never said a word, not even now. He stood there in the sun, gazing straight ahead and soaking up responsibility. Now I should write how I felt that moment as though there were nobody else in the whole world but us. Mustachio, who never bows his head, Jana, who lives in perpetual warfare and doesn't want to die, the medic with the forgotten name who came out of the woods and did his duty, Frenk, with bullet wounds in his legs and the nightmare that he might be dying that very minute and the reality that he probably was, and Diego and I, who as yet hadn't gotten caught up in the fear. But back then the symbolic or whatever didn't occur to any of us, we just remained silent, and Diego and Jana clicked their shutters a couple of times, force of habit.

Then finally the ambulances arrived screaming, toiled their way past the tanks, and the medics picked up the ones who looked rescuable to them. Two photographers dashed up from somewhere, clicking away, then ran back. In the woods two wounded guys from the territorial defense force were loaded into the ambulances. We dragged the dead into the shade and covered them. We put the clean bandages that were left lying on the ground in our pockets, in case we needed them later. End of scene.

THIRD FIGHT. It was very noisy by the house. Everybody was still in shock and discussing the air-raid. Most of the people didn't have the faintest idea what had actually happened up front where the Turks were. Diego and I didn't feel like shedding any light, we just wanted to wash the blood away. We were all so damn happy we'd stayed alive. Proud we'd stayed alive. It was important that we'd stayed alive. One of the neighbors told everyone who'd listen how only one roof-tile was damaged, everything else had remained intact. The only one who understood was the grandma. She knew about wars. She scolded her daughter and son-in-law for leaving their children elsewhere. "When a thing like this happens, you gotta stay together, all four of you," she told them, "so that if it gets you, you all go together."

What then was the result of all this? The only thing that stood in the tanks' way was the train. And the train was the one thing the planes had missed. The line of trucks wasn't in the way at all, but they blew it to bits, as they did the bushes on the other side of the road. When the planes came the second time it wasn't that bad. They somehow didn't feel like shooting any more, and they aimed the missiles better. They hit the train, but only the boxcars, not the frame. Thus they failed to move the train out of the way, and the tanks eventually tried to go around it on both sides. During this, one tank got stuck in the mud, another was stranded in the brook, and the entire operation was regressing into a farce.

The remaining six tanks now had a clear path all the way to the border except for the last dozen trucks at the intersection at Šentilj, and Diego and I retreated to that last patch. We set up camp behind the duty-free shop past the check-point gate, saved our last two cigarettes and stared at the *wilkommen* sign for foreign tourists at the Habakuk Hotel. The Austrians behind our backs were on the lookout with binoculars, our policemen in front of us were wearing bullet-proof vests and unhappy faces and getting psyched up for the final combat. Beside that, there were still army snipers in the blockhouse on the hill, and everyone was looking for cover. We were tired and fell asleep on the blacktop.

When we awoke, we were still hopelessly cut off from everything. So we crossed over into Austria. We must have been a sight, me in shorts I hadn't changed, Diego with his sleep-deprived Argentine face. We explained we wanted to stay there awhile, and they let us in even though I didn't have my passport on me. Phone connections with Ljubljana were down, behind the border various displaced Balkanites were eating *cevapcici* all over the place, and all we could get in those dumb stores selling cheap coffee was bananas and juice. Then Jana also came to mail her rolls of film from there. Diego was making plans how he'd sneak his photos past the army and into Ljubljana.

And then as though we'd summoned him, Krainer, the governor of Steiermark, pulled up in a limo, and Diego and Jana explained what had happened. He listened kindly, with a smile pasted on his face, and then with a handshake drove off. We left in the opposite direction, to get the end of the story.

THE END. Somehow, there was no end. First, talk of a cease-fire started, the tanks stood there in the road a kilometer from the border crossing, the soldiers had climbed out and they were young and they wanted to go home, and one of them shot himself in the foot. We went over to Belna's for some cucumber soup on the house, Belna opened his restaurant especially for us, music played in the background, and all we really wanted was to unwind. It had been one long day.

Too long to relax. Waiting in the car the whole night and watching the woods on the other side where commando paratroopers had dug in, and behind them the territorial defense. The journey back, Ormož, crossing the Drava over a dam, sentries on a hill, speeding in Ljubljana, head ducked low. Making a choice. Two worlds. One asking when this was all going to end. And the other. Wrong question. Wrong thinking. Be ready. Think about what is important. One world with the press conference about a polit- ical solution to the problems. The other with the army in Središče ob Dravi, where they made us turn back in our car, destroyed ten fortunately empty rolls of film, and let us by only because we shouted back at them. A world with the bridge of brotherhood and unity in Ormož burned down. With the boy in the nearby bush sweating at the thought of shooting at another boy in a tank. Thinking the nonsense away. One world with the fear they'd start shelling. The other with Jana laughing that if a community isn't ready to sac- rifice lives it ain't worth it. Both worlds so alive. Both so understandable. Both so unjust. We're going out again tomorrow, to look for closure.

Translated by Tamara Soban.

POETRY

Edvard Kocbek

The Lippizaners

A newspaper reports:
the Lippizaners collaborated
on an historical film.
A radio explains:
a millionaire had bought the Lippizaners,
the noble animals were quiet
throughout the journey over the Atlantic.
And a textbook teaches:
the Lippizaners are graceful riding horses,
their origin is in the Karst, they are of supple hoof,
conceited trot, intelligent nature
and obstinate fidelity.

But I have to add, my son,
that it isn't possible to fit these
restless animals into any set pattern:
it is good, when the day shines,
the Lippizaners are black foals.
And it is good, when the night reigns,
the Lippizaners are white mares,
but the best is,
when the day comes out of the night,
then the Lippizaners are white and black buffoons,
the court fools of its Majesty,
Slovenian history.

Others have worshipped holy cows and dragons,
thousand-year-old turtles and winged lions,
unicorns, double-headed eagles and phoenixes,
but we've chosen the most beautiful animal,
which proved to be excellent on battlefields, in circuses,

harnessed to princesses and the Golden Monstrance,
therefore the emperors of Vienna spoke
French with skillful diplomats,
Italian with charming actresses,
Spanish with the infinite God,
and German with uneducated servants:
but with the horses they talked Slovenian.

Remember, my child, how mysteriously
nature and history are bound together,
and how different are the driving forces of the spirit
of each of the world's peoples.
You know well that ours is the land of contests and races.
You, thus, understand why the white horses
from Noah's Ark found a refuge on our pure ground,
why they became our holy animal,
why they entered into the legend of history,
and why they bring the life pulse to our future.
They incessantly search for our promised land
and are becoming our spirit's passionate saddle.

I endlessly sit on a black and white horse,
my beloved son,
like a Bedouin chieftain
I blend with my animal,
I've been traveling on it all my life,
I sleep on it, and I dream on it
and I'll die on it.
I learned all our prophesies
on that mysterious animal,
and this poem, too, I experienced
on its trembling back.

Nothing is darker than
clear speech,
and nothing is more true than a poem,

which the intellect cannot seize,
heroes limp in the bright sun
and sages stammer in the dark,
the buffoons, though, are changing into poets,
the winged Pegasi run faster and faster
above the caves of our old earth
jumping and pounding—
the impatient Slovenian animals
are still trying to awaken King Matjaž.

Those who don't know how to ride a horse
should learn quickly
how to tame the fiery animal,
how to ride freely in a light saddle,
how to catch the harmony of the trot,
and above all to persist in the premonition,
for our horses came galloping from far away,
and they still have far to go:
motors tend to break down,
elephants eat too much,
our road is a long one,
and it is too far to walk.

Song About Man

Incapable of being, except in our body, collected, girded, suffering force:

Each of us convulsively clings to himself, even asleep we contract like
worms under stones.

Something always compels us, we vibrate in all directions, and at rest
we are perplexed.

The longer we live, the more we are tangled in gravity, we acknowledge
encounters only when they have passed.

We pulse constantly, the human race contains limitless movements,
whatever occurs is completing itself.

Wind tires us, a song makes us anxious, a tree unsettles us, the earth
puts us to sleep.

Looking is marveling, running is fear, solitude is nostalgia and speech
solemn vows.

Extending beyond our own selves, time sips, space extends us, we are
stretched taut on the earth's magnetic field.

When we come together we are drunk with each other, our faces are
changed, someone else is among us.

When suffering lets go we look at our hands and play with them, we lift
them, reverently moving the fingers, each of them equally dear.

In the expanse of the world we are a trembling of leaves or the shadows
of clouds over brightly colored hills.

We cannot abide by either morning or evening, at noon we deny
ourselves, and at night we shiver from strangeness.

We can find neither beginning nor end in ourselves, in the great
silence we hear perpetual music and bow our heads.

We are placed among lines and figures for convenience's sake, some are
horizontal, others stand vertical, it is assuring to grasp them.

Objects jut silently into space, maintaining their taut forms. They
neither collapse nor contract, they will endure to the end with us.

Outside animals respire, their meekness overwhelms us, and in their
huge eyes we lose our balance.

Everything is the foundation of what is higher, the crown to what is lower,
bindweed to whatever is at hand.

The mark of man is in dualities that attract and affirm one another,

the game outruns its own speed.
The transitions and joints make sense of each other like a word pronounced
    in the ear, truth seethes like a troubled ocean.
We move our bodies ritually and deliberately like priests chanting,
    each side gives way, humility and splendor complete one another.
Man's heart beats audibly, it hears and deciphers more all the time, man's
    heart is one fruit among many, the tithe from the harvest of dying time.
Each thing in its proper place, earth and sea, night and day, sorrow
    and joy, oblivion and the gift, within them man, unique.

Slovenian Hymn

Small and meek. I grow into the cosmic order, my brothers speak the same
    words as I, lifted from idleness, we gaze at the sphere of the earth.
The earth has been neatly drawn, the ground is indomitable, we set up
    our white houses long ago and bordered them in blue.
Its furrowed surface is worked into a wistful sky, live dark belts encircle it,
    all measures have banded wisely together.
Streams purl over the earth and springs gurgle, forests susurrate, fields
    sprawl in tacit persistence, flies swarm in the sunlight,
    gnats over twilit paths.
From village to village it is neither too far nor too near, enclosed gardens
    surround the homesteads, a dark green hedge looks out over a fence.
Fruit trees ripen around the houses, the wind prowls in their branches,
    a steep trail leads up to vineyeards, down to a cellar where mallet blows
    thud dully.
Huge wardrobes stand in the parlors, the wall clock's pendulum chats
    with eternity, a cat kneads by the oven and apricot trees blossom
    in the soft grass below the fields.
The sun illuminates the great altar at evening, mass and the people's
    singing blend with incense, while now and then a schoolboy drops his
    hat.
Girls wear white kerchiefs to vespers, a flower pressed in the prayer-book
    of each, and during the way of the cross they glance at the acolytes in
    black.
Pigeons cluck in the graveyard chapel, bats hang in the church tower,
    bees have their hive by the stream and mushrooms grow in places only
    old wives know.
Modest plum and apple trees flower in fertile ground, grain billows over
    gentle hillsides and flatlands, an occasional fish leaps out of the frothy
    water.
Fields of dry gold lie benumbed in the summer heat, shepherds light
    fires in high autumn meadows, a song about vineyards resounds amid
    strokes of mallets.
We dance at banquets and listen to a comical fiddler, and as we sort
    through seeds by a warm stove the wind and a creaky wagon strapped

with chains go past together.

Experience dozes on the hay and in forests, love stirs in distracted
young boys, candles burn at graves and bells chime at midnight mass.

The holidays range from All Souls to Corpus Christi and Marymas,
buckwheat follows wheat, turnips barley, we set out potatoes in the
fallows, clover grows wild among the wheat.

People are like ants in the fields and on hillsides, at times a voice calls
from the distance, which another one answers.

Asleep, there is a flicker of the thought of work, during work hope
smolders, hope is tinged with sadness, then churchbells ring again.

Lifted from our idleness we gaze at the earth's sphere, and lo, the more
deeply we stare, the heavier the deepness, stunned with pain we taste
the bitterness of roots.

And look, smoke sweeps the horizon, swallows look plaintively from
their nests, a bronze bell has cracked down the middle.

In silence mothers rock their children, potters' wheels stop, fabric rips
on the loom, day laborers have bent their backs for years.

O land of our fathers, given to us like an enchanted princess, when
will you be saved?

You are our night phantom, our morning burden, midday muddle and
evening sadness, holy redemption wells up within us.

Disowned, you endure, great mother, quietly calling us, you have been
ravaged, fertile body, and your children put to shame.

Our footsteps cry out to you, our kinship and comfort, we lift up our
hands from your ancient soil and answer.

At night your eyes open like a passionflower, you take count of us,
beside your hearth our souls beat as one.

You are the ark of our covenant, which we guard, we must be watchful
each night and sing the songs we are pledged to.

O fearsome ripening of the ageless secret, unspeakably strong wine,
we sense you in our blood, we are drunk like young fathers.

Hands

I've lived between my hands
as though between two thieves.
Neither has ever known
what the other intended.
My left hand was witless from compassion,
my right adept at everything.
One would grasp, the other let slip,
they assiduously hid from each other
and performed all their tasks halfway.

Today, as I was running from death,
falling and getting up, and falling,
dragging myself through thorns and over rocks,
both of my hands were equally bloody.
I extended them like two sacrificial branches
of some great temple candelabrum,
which bore witness with equal ardor.
Belief and disbelief became a single flame
which shot up hot and high.

Into the Dark

And when I stretch my hands into the darkness
gently, cautiously, lovingly,
I know that I am close to you,
and then I start to call you softly,
endlessly, you who were,
who are, who will be yet again;
and look, my calling brings you close
and your presence starts to fill
the limitless darkness,
where the distances are short
and everything is tangible, though unseen.

I call more quietly
and more sincerely
and suddenly you're here,
when I move my hands again
in the irritable darkness
my fingers discover you,
I recognize your shapes
and know that you are here
and that I can never
again neglect you.

Who Am I?

I never am
what people think I am,
and never where
eyes see me.
Enemies say that I'm
the heir apparent,
my friends maintain that I'm
a covert monk,
and wags would have me
rotting in the log
of a sunken vessel
that sought new lands.
But I kneel down at noon
and etch dictations of silence
in the desert sand,
toward evening gnash my teeth
in a dangerous crevice
of the tower of Babel,
and at night lie meekly down
among the swords
on Hamlet's terrace.
Only toward morning
do I swing up in the horizon's saddle
at the farthest corner of the world
and set out to find
the generous rose
ready to erupt.
One day it will look
this arrogant century in the face
and the century will blush.

My Life

At first I knew how to pray and shark,
only later did I take up drawing and writing,
that's when I was seized with dizziness.
I rocked between the past tense
and its past perfect form,
an oversized hat kept falling over my eyes,
and the transfixed kid lay sprawled across the grass.

The sky showed its four corners,
I searched out Attila, met the miller's daughter,
sighted fires from the church tower at night.
In mad company I was set on the table
and made to perform a water sprite.
In the shrubs I caught sight of bodies convulsing.
The strange play of two of them moved me.

It was then that my homeland left me,
I set my wooden suitcase down in a foreign kitchen,
each day I set the compass point in my heart,
and the circles kept getting more acute.
I planned escapes, conspiracies, sinlessness,
my first poem turned into a trapeze and
I leapt into the world like a flea from the sphinx's fur.

I shut the logarithms and opened dream atlases,
discovered green monks and trails over the earth,
sailed into a gulf, hopped trains,
in the Parisian darkness spotted a glazier.
The time of gold-toothed thieves had begun.
At the Fig Tree the Penates had dispersed,
death danced naked amid knives.

Then they sent me into history
as a child is sent after bird's milk.

I was seized, they threw me in a clearing,
and it was there coincidence shamed me.
I survived, changed into a monster,
dragged up to the wall of the city
cowering before Mandarin lust.

Still the pranksters hadn't had enough.
They lined me up with long-distance runners,
no one knew who held the secret message.
And when all of us—different, impatient—tore
off through the endless arena collecting laps,
at one point I lagged so far behind the most powerful
that I suddenly came out ahead of them.

The Time of Poems

They say the time of poems is passing,
man has sold all his surplus,
deficiencies are tiring,
the fear of death is demolishing
poetics after poetics,
what we write are just signs,
only a fool eats what isn't there.

We are all in an exhausted space.
Time sets and rises again.
Every darkness is a miracle,
every muddle is a cure.
Violence and unease are relentless.
Our native land has gone abroad
like a girl before a mirror,
delighted with her own face.
The sea is enormously deep.

Now I'm coming back, my dearest.
The gardener's open hand glows with charms.
She never repeats the gesture.
I copy her by tattooing
everything that lives and lose my fear.
The ravings of an idiom beyond belief
steam from the seven wounds of holy folly.
I leave through ravaged regions.
I have let all my fields lie fallow.
My queen is still out pollinating.
You will know me by my bare feet
and deep dreams of a mountain
that went to the prophet.

"We walk, exhausted and dimly changed"

We walk, exhausted and dimly changed.
None of us remembers where or when, but
somewhere we sang around a poplar and slept beneath
steep hills; sometimes we go downward as though
for night work at a mill, at others we climb up,
as if expected at a winepress.

A windmill jerks, its faint creaking follows
us down the valley floor. There is no center to this
dark space, I constantly strain forward,
my loved one is far off. A cold shudder courses through
my body, how much I would like to see her smartly, autumnally
dressed, ready for a night journey, we have so far yet to go.

Translated by Michael Biggins.

Jože Udovič

And Yet

And yet, throw nothing away.
Everywhere are hidden signs,
look behind the rotting fence, the wooden wall,
the old picture, into the empty jug,
behind solitude's door, inside the ruined house,
beneath a heap of ashes, beneath the fire's corpse,
beneath a calloused hand, beneath the roots of words,
beneath a stone, into a wound, into the face of fear,
at wasted pastures, behind a solitary bush,
somewhere a shelter is hidden, as yet unknown,
a gentle womb of poems and feathers,
of azure moss and breath
which may give rise
to an unheard-of harmony.

Little Night Music

Stars, and sky's crickets,
sang in night's meadow; as it approached,
it passed a burning bush,
its footsteps echoing
in the valley of the moon.

It came in clothing
woven from fragile birdsong,
and in the wind's cut-glass shoes.

And it lit candles,
changed one to a child,
a traveler, a gardener;
a white windmill clanked in its voice,
its eyes were dark
saffron with gold powder,
and its heart
a diving swallow.

The Boat

Let me stay
this night far out,
alone upon the swelling wave,
upon the wave that changes darkly
everything that breathes.
And in the boat of change
I'll play, in the boat of desire
carrying it off,
on the wave of shadow, which is cold,
on the reflection which weaves at night
long wreaths
and hangs them on the marked man's
neck. Let me stay
with the night, without illusions,
on the wave
that seeks no shores,
in the boat of the shadow that carries it off,
not knowing
where it will land.

Translated by Michael Biggins.

November

The house shrank into itself
And on the forehead
New frowns appeared;
In the swept doorway sit
Dull saints from the calendar,
They opened the box and beheld
The mildewed grains of life;
Through shuttered windows come
The damp, dark hours;
The invisible wings flap
On the sighing chimney;
The door vibrates
In the deadly draft.
The shadow is already in the house,
The shadow is in the house.
The hands of him
Who looks at her
Eye to eye
Became chapped at the last minute
Like tree bark;
The muddy water of images
Blurred in front of his eyes.
In the stove the flame shrieks
Like a scared animal.
The trees with crooked fingers
Cross out November in the air,
And in the house a blind face on a pillow
Turned up to the rotten ceiling.

Image of an Unreal Place—A Sketch

The wind sighs, shut in a cage in the square,
There are cracks in the walls like petrified lightning,
Old women bring to the church black lilies of loneliness,
In the morning streams of darkness flow down the streets
Carrying with them bits of cries.

In the Street of Loneliness there are a few mad princes,
In whitewashed houses they play at kings,
Shrouded in gold stage costumes,
And in front of their door
People express their requests
To the servant, who is deaf and dumb.
Occasionally a torrent suddenly rushes
And carries away a child or a woman
And no one notices
Someone is gone.

In the dark nights a piano can be heard
In the depths of the sea;
Low humming voices,
And the princes and servants
Close their ears
And fall asleep.

When the north wind blows,
The owls display the beheaded moon
On the church roof
And bats deliver
From house to house
The threatening letters of night.

Translated by Igor Maver.

Dane Zajc

You Are Not

You are not in the voice of the wind, not in the diffusion of the mountains,
you are not in the blossoms, and if the birds beckon, they do not beckon
    to you,
you are not in the nakedness of the earth, not in the languid odor
    of the grass,
and if you plant roses, to smell of you, they smell of themselves,
and if you lay a road, the road will narrate its own story,
and if you build a home, if you fill it with precious things, it will one day
    take you in like a stranger
and the things will talk to themselves in their own language, mocking you.

It is a lie that the spring exists only to quench your thirst, that the river
    exists only to bathe you in its cool embrace.
It is a lie that objects exist only to soothe you with peaceful memories,
because one day your whole world will oppose you.

One day the objects will change their names,
the stones will hate, the wind will threaten,
the street will frighten, the birds will hammer your brow
with the searing nails of their voices, the river will be despair,
your possessions will be your guilt and your accusers.
The world will be in ruins. The world will have no name.

But then you will not care. You will sit in a forsaken corner.
You will close your eyes and see nothing. Most of all you won't see
your own bewilderment in the bewildered and deserted world.
So that you won't think that you must
do something, that you must walk somewhere with your legs,
which will be spindly like the legs of a black spider.
Only your head will be big. Your head will blossom
white like a magnolia. You will search long in the white cave of your

mouth for a name for yourself,
but this time, better than to find a name for going on,
would be to find a name for the end.

Rain

The cadavers of memory grow quickly in the night
as rain falls upon the barren patches of their graves,
though your past won't comfort you in the least.
And the rats which abandoned your ship
proved long ago that you are already sinking.
Surely and inevitably.

Rain exists for itself, not falling through your thoughts because of you.
In the long nights, locomotives pass through you,
beckoning your memory, pulling it into the wide expanse
that you don't like to visit.
Perhaps you will withdraw into a slumber quilted with rain.
It really won't matter at all:
in the morning, you will awaken before a mountain of refuse
you have to crawl over:
you will want to see the insignificant plain on the other side of the mountain,
to see if anything there has changed.
But nothing ever changes.
Always a soft grayness bereft of the passing years.
And the path upon which a woman flees. Beautiful and fickle, like a bird
someone has tried long and unsuccessfully to kill.
And you know, she will always flee like that.
In front of her is a wall of grayness and behind her, you, riddled
with the hollow voices of the locomotives passing through your nights.

The rainy night doesn't live without you.
You recognize the cadavers conveyed upon night's glassy rope
and you despise their contempt.
They want to take even your misery away.
You frighten them with their skulls.

You're safe in the rainy night.
Hidden and alone in a great head of rain
like a chrysalis in the heart of the mountain.

Dead Things

Rain lapped at the stones.
Water stands in the hearth.
Rain wears away the oven.
Sand fills the cellar.

The vines grow wild.
The well crumbles.
The last wall collapses.

Thistles grow in the corner,
where the table once stood.
Quiet evening conversation,
father's elbow on the table.
Dead father.

Your elbow has decayed.
Your hand is soil.

Who will tame the vines.
Who will light the fire.
Who will dig up from beneath the hearth
the decaying faces of dead years.

Dead Pines

We were shrunken from fear.
We were roots grabbing at the earth.
And it approached us, night's anxious face.

The mountain's brow crushed us.
Buried us with stones.
Flogged us with voices.

The skin fell away from us.
Our bones became tangled together.
Our roots grabbed for air.

Our bodies thrashed by the sun,
the twisted desire:
to have green needles.
A leafy green crown.

In death, our image was severe.
Bony and gray told the story:
death is the blow.
Death is the body's maelstrom.
A battle beneath still dark waters.

Safeguard your eyes.
Close the doors of your hearing
before our silence.

From *Two*

The ice of her body melts
under his hands.
The fruits of autumn stir beneath his fingers.
The autumn of her body.
Your body has the fragrance
of moss under fruit, he tells her.

And when he tells her this,
two forests of stubborn thoughts
flee to two sides of the sky.

Two caressing hands tear down
the rocky wall erected between their eyes.
I am drunk on your legs, he tells her.
I am dust on the rainbow of your breath,
she answers him.
My body is christened in your scent,
she whispers to him.

Peaceful, they lie side by side.
And deep, deep within them murmur
two forests chained to the ice.
But they lie upon the silent surface.
So still that they can hear
the high, high dam growing between them.
And the cold water falling across the dam.

Translated by Erica Johnson Debeljak.

Gregor Strniša

There Was a Tiger Here

I.

A bright spring rain fell the day through.
The branches drip, the sand in the lanes is damp yet.
The sky has cleared. Slowly you go through the park,
the sun of evening haunts it, apparitionlike.

In the illumined peak of the dark tree,
a blackbird sings and sings. The evening's very quiet.
The sunlight turns wine red. And on the lawn,
there shimmers a bronze monument.

Just then you spot in the wet ground before you,
the wide, the clear, the deep impressions.
The park is very big, sunstriped, and full of shadows.
You start, go on, but know: a tiger came this way.

II.

You still remember the day
when first you saw the tiger's trail.
You had just woken, and there it was.
Morning was like evening, full of shadows.

That was oh so long ago.
The night of that morning, you lay alert in the dark,
then fell into mazy sleep, like gazing out a window
and beyond it softly snows and will not stop.

You live as if not much has changed, really.
Soon after that morning, autumn came,

then we had the long, the damp winter,
and wet snow covered a dark city.

III.

You sit, elbows on the table, you look out the window.
It is later afternoon, soon to be dusk.
Not a sound will come into the room now.
You think how, outside, the winter day is fading.

You see just a piece of the sky and a roof, it is red,
likely the snow slid from it in the noontime sun.
In the last of light, the chimney casts a feeble shadow.
Evening will be leadblue, you think, and a little foggy.

You go to the window. A woman in white walks in the street,
across the way a child plays in the sand,
a summer day flickers in the darkened trees.
Like a great shimmering cloud, fades the summer day.

IV.

Maybe not much has changed, at all.
It's just that in rooms where once you were already,
you fail to find a favorite picture on a wall,
now there's only a pale rectangle there.

More and more often on your familiar routes,
tall, dusty horsemen cross your path.
Places you walk in, day after day,
bronze heavy monuments suddenly occupy.

And sometimes, entering a familiar house,
you find yourself in a cellar, stale and squat.
It was not there before. And huge snarling dogs
are tearing at their chains outside in the gardens.

V.

So you live, you're always off to distant places,
down foggy seas, up snowy mountain ranges,
you see so many new, so many foreign cities,
in whose small quiet squares you love to sit.

There, too, on the smooth pavement, from time to time,
dark, broad stripes stand out in the slanting sun.
You pick up a stone, you weigh it in your palm,
you murmur absently: There was a tiger here.

But him, himself, you haven't met yet.
Whoever the tiger looks at soon dies.
Always he pads before you, through summer's dark door,
through the white, fog chambers beneath December's skies.

Snow

They're not eternal, these heavens,
these absent galaxies,
not eternal, this blue star forlorn—
only we mourn.

We mourn as a small creature,
in the hills, sometimes, mourns away,
except that maybe our hurt is deeper:
will the memory stay?

Will the two of you ever, in memory, here,
as you did, live again—will the memory go?
Will you be, at least, without the memory, together?
Will she, will you know?

Translated by Tom Ložar.

From *The Inferno:*

Part II. - The Mountain

1.

Its two peaks are never obscured by mists.
The highest crags are clearly visible.
No one can say why, but still it seems
that mists perpetually enfold the mountain.

The sky is blue, without the slightest cloud.
The sand is yellow. It glows dully in the sun.
The desert all around is flat to the horizons.
The mountain, like the smell of dirt, is black.

It juts up from the plain like the fist of a giant
that lies mostly buried deep in sand,
at dusk it's like the head of a bull's carcass,
its forehead broad and flat, with hollow eyes.

3.

The wind is chained to the mountain like a wolf,
while silence wails in its depths.
Whoever enters it goes groping blindly
through the long, low trenches of the labyrinth.

Many wander into dead-end passageways.
Trapped in the narrows, they die of thirst and hunger.
Each of them starts raving in his death throes,
imagining he's living as he did before:

inviting friends to banquets, or picking
cool spheres of fruit from dewy trees.
The last echo of his own delirious laughter

falls like a white mask onto his lifeless face.

5.

In the mountain's depths, in its far-off heart,
in the final, narrowest chamber of the labyrinth,
the Minotaur stands waiting in the lofty dark.
Delirium's creature: human, with a bull's dark head.

Whatever happens here takes place in silence—
an encounter in a land of endless night,
a sudden recollection of a distant morning, snowy white,
an eye that glimpses you, but which you don't notice.

Only very few attain these regions.
And none of them has come back from the mountain.
Some perish in the maze from thirst and hunger,
the Minotaur impales the others on its horns.

Translated by Michael Biggins.

Kajetan Kovič

A Poem

How difficult it is to part
With a poem
Which you made love to for at least one night.
How much more difficult than the one that
Was burning in your hands
For many an evening,
And has accompanied you with an unfinished step
Through many springs.
You built her out of air
That was vanishing along the way,
From the quicksand in the wind
And the boundless sea,
Which was herself.
You saw the invisible,
You heard, lashed to the mast,
That which murders and kills,
And you still survived
Because of her mercy.
What could these wretched hands do,
What this wretched ink,
What these wretched candles,
What this wretched night—
Without her sweet whip,
Which promises a victory to this lagging horse
In a race that can never be won.

Translated by Igor Maver.

Dead Soldiers' Autumn

The leaves are falling now

As we ourselves that autumn season fell
Among the somber leaves of history.
For glory of one homeland or another
We laid ourselves, to order, down to rot.

Passerby, do not stop. Here rest
Duties unspecified but now fulfilled
And so discharged from loyalty and life.

No, passerby, remembrance pays no ransom.
Our death remains. So do not feel your way
To final desperation in our dust:

Above us, look,

New blades of grass are growing;
But out of us there cannot grow again
So much as one root to one blade of grass
And if there is some homeland somewhere still,
The day when we could die for it is done.

Translated by Alasdair MacKinnon.

Garden of Gold

The chill and the damp under the pines.
The long shadow over the dark house.
Grapes, blue as dreams.
In curtained rooms,
dying fathers,
whose punishment is sons
left behind in wars,
entranced by the cuckoos' singing.
In the garden, the yellow autumn hour,
and under sweaters,
the warm breasts of girls,
as they lie down horizontal
under the curiosity of boys,
and as above them, blue as death,
ripens the isabella.

Rain

Rain is making a racket in the gutter,
an insistent, wistful, tinny hum,
spread across the acacias,
across their intense, waiting scents.
The dogs stare vacantly at the yellow horizon.
They scent the hunt, and the wet, alien animal.
A mild evening is on its way.
The wall is sticky and sweating.
The boys stroke the wet dogs
and their own tight unknown bodies.

Labrador

White is the river's roar
in Labrador's dark taigas.
Far away the foggy shore.
With hills between. And seas.

There is the pine wood solitary.
There is the breath of place, perpetual.
There is the fragrant, resiny bark.
There is the ripe, red berry.

There are the green lights of the cypresses,
spread out the dawn.
There are the fires of southern stars.
And hills and seas, and on and on.

Translated by Tom Ložar.

Veno Taufer

The Fish Faronika Carries the World on Her Back

faronika fish
swims through the sea

gnawed to her tail
faronika fish

jesus catch
jesus multiply

because of the gray depths
because of the big and the little fish

Translated by Elisavietta Ritchie.

The Kangaroo

the kangaroo never sleeps
the sun rises from the belly of the kangaroo

the kangaroo frightens the maps of the world
with the belly full of sun it rattles

the kangaroo jumps over the seas of the world
with the belly full of sun it rattles

the sun goes down in the belly of the kangaroo
the kangaroo jumps up to the sky
with the belly full of night it rattles

Translated by Michael Scammell.

Into Your Eye

it is not in the foam in the wake of the ship
adrift though starry plankton it is when
drought and sand blow into nostrils
it is under anything possible
which has the voice of pulleys it is not in wax
nor in signs at the crossroads it is not when
the dusty city lies underfoot and in the pestilent door
no dust can be found on the threshold it is
not when you look around and inside it is
in the gust sweeping a lash into your eye

Translated by Elisavietta Ritchie.

Wind

from the south you bring rain
you haul in the trees
someone has hanged himself
you subside into calm

you who lash weather vanes
you who topple haystacks
you who spread stink carry a voice
who bring hail marries turncoats

windmill sail
flame on the rooftop
plague breaths flower seeds
blow blow

Translated by Michael Scammell.

Svetlana Makarovič

Anthill

I.

All the same. I am the same.
You are the same. All of us.
Our larders full. Never enough.
We need more. Don't like strangers.
That are different. No.
Or light in the kitchen. Eye on the door.
We have. To have. Will have.
The same. It's good. It's right. Don't think.

II.

This day I'm a whoop.
The wind airs my downy feathers.
I'll sing and fly, my death
will be a drop of forest air
for the bright wind to drink.
The great forest shines and shines.
At nightfall I expand into a huge predator,
and my sharp beak glows golden.

III.

In the big house there are people living.
They whelp plump children, satisfaction.
They stare at blind mirrors and nod.
Their eyes are neat, big buttons
that they fasten and undo.
They seize their things with hands.
They don't know about the golden beak—
opening above their roof.

The Snake

I.

Like a noble fire,
poison flares in it.
It winds through smoldering stones—
a slender, cold sovereign.
Stretching out in the sun's palm,
and staring in its face.
It kills every shadow
that falls across its pure body.
Aspiring to be a golden skeleton
when fall returns.

II.

It shuns returning to darkness.
It dreams of dancing
slow, sad dances;
its shadow is gold in the dark.
Poison blazes in it,
green and bright.
It wears no masks.
Each night holds up to it an awful mirror.
Each night wraps a black chain tight around its neck.
Each night it keeps watch, black, heavy in damp sand,
awaiting the distant sun.
Its flat grimace growing more and more bitter.

III.

It danced a grim dance of death
on a pile of stones.
The sun withdrew its hands.
September breathed through the grass.

It went taut as a spear and collapsed.
It had wanted to be a gold skeleton
when fall returned.
But when fall came it was
just a blasted branch in the bleary air.
The grater of summer would
never consume it to the end.

Translated by Michael Biggins.

Niko Grafenauer

Fatigue

Winds bloat on the branches like a long restrained urge.
Silently you sink into the shadow-streaked forest
where winter petrifies the birds tearing themselves to pieces
for their bleary significance, your spirit circles like a baby monkey.

It is growing dark, the gallows stand like an empty door in your mind,
its shadow falls in your way. Fatigue looms behind your back;
if you glance across your shoulder, evil phantoms arise;
the waste country before you greens with spreading mould.

I Am

Noon at mid-summer is cruel as clear consciousness.
Whatever escapes numbness only in form is cut for prey,
Snakes twirl upward like wisps of smoke.
It is growing dark, autumn is distant and drawing near.

With the laws of the dead I established freedom
in order to subdue it and ascertain everything.
Winds girdle me, it's a long climb.
The pain that I am enters into me like a knife.

Behind me full of evil composure lurks silence.
The fall is long like an outcry that dies in the distance.
Lost in silence I seek strength for a new venture,
but everything seems to rot in the grip of darkness.

The House

The house where you think things over
is growing tense like a darkening day.
Memories close in
as if you were dying with gloomy dignity.

Silence shines upon the immobility
you take from the dead.
Loneliness gnaws you like verdigris.

In the narrow crack of permitted consciousness
projecting itself like a beam into dusk,
moths quiver.
Love throws your enlarged shadow against the wall.
With a clammy key I step toward the threshold.
I call from the verge of black forebodings
into emptiness.
Silence is your language.
        I grow quiet,
but within me, as in late autumn,
sounds flutter, almost tears.
The house where you think things over
is like the beginning of all that goes away.

Translated by Jože Lazar.

Tomaž Šalamun

History

Tomaž Šalamun is a monster.
Tomaž Šalamun is a sphere rushing through the air.
He lies down in twilight, he swims in twilight.
People and I, we both look at him amazed,
we wish him well, maybe he is a comet.
Maybe he is punishment from the gods,
the boundary stone of the world.
Maybe he is such a speck in the universe
that he will give energy to the planet
when oil, steel, and food run short.
He might only be a hump, his head
should be taken off like a spider's.
But then something would then suck up
Tomaž Šalamun, possibly the head.
Possibly he should be pressed between
glass, his photo should be taken.
He should be put in formaldehyde, so children
would look at him as they do at fetuses,
protei, and mermaids.
Next year, he'll probably be in Hawaii
or in Ljubljana. Doorkeepers will scalp
tickets. People walk barefoot
to the university there. The waves can be
a hundred feet high. The city is fantastic,
shot through with people on the make,
the wind is mild.
But in Ljubljana people say: look!
This is Tomaž Šalamun, he went to the store
with his wife Maruška to buy some milk.
He will drink it and this is history.

Translated by Bob Perelman and the author.

Jonah

how does the sun set?
like snow
what color is the sea?
large
Jonah are you salty?
I'm salty
Jonah are you a flag?
I'm a flag
the fireflies rest now

what are stones like?
green
how do little dogs play?
like flowers
Jonah are you a fish?
I'm a fish
Jonah are you a sea urchin?
I'm a sea urchin
listen to the flow

Jonah is the roe running through the woods
Jonah is the mountain breathing
Jonah is all the houses
have you ever heard such a rainbow?
what is the dew like?
are you asleep?

Translated by Elliot Anderson and the author.

Folk Song

Every true poet is a monster.
He destroys people and their speech.
His singing elevates a technique that wipes out
the earth so we are not eaten by worms.
The drunk sells his coat.
The thief sells his mother.
Only the poet sells his soul to separate it
from the body that he loves.

Death's Window

To stop the blood of flowers and rotate the order of things.
To die in the river, to die in the river.
To hear the heart of the rat. There's no difference
Between the moon's and my tribe's silver.

To clean the field and run as far as the earth's edge.
To carry in my breast the word: the crystal. At the door
The soap's evaporating, the conflagration lit up the day.
To turn around, to turn around once more.

And to strip the frock. The poppy had bitten through the sky.
To walk the desert roads and drink shadows.
To feel the oak tree in the mouth of a spring.

To stop the blood of flowers, to stop the blood of flowers.
The altars look at each other, eye to eye.
To lie down on a blue cabbage.

Translated by Charles Simic.

Red Cliff

Gently, gently as you can,
as you hear, as you know.
Darkly, darkly as you fall,
as you shine and as you eat.

Let the flies return to their hive.
Up with your hands, golden city.
Helmets glint, the sun goes down,
the terraced gardens calming down

and cooling. And when you draw back
the oar to keep from denting the pier,
fear not. You won't hit a thing.
You'll be a church. You'll be cloth. It's how you are.

I and Thou

Your lips have never kissed me, you've never
drunk snow. You melancholy moment, frigid
under these snowdrifts. Let me ask a cruel question—
do you still heat your igloo? I cast a spell on you

and tore your limbs off. And those creases deepening
in what was once a godlike brow, perhaps you've even lost
your right to them. You haven't hurt me more, you haven't.
Little mummy, aborted flower, the memory of you fades.

Oceans divide us, and you're jaded. The hard stone
hopeless, smeared with silicate. We shall yet make love,
and I shall grease those beehives yet. My desire has weakened

now, you've won, you are indeed a void. And I,
the tree-lined path of countless others, contain your red heart,
gone rigid, too. I have gurgled with happiness only in you.

Translated by Michael Biggins.

Versailles

The borders of the countries on the earth's crust
hold less than the frostwork on my window. The tree
gets dressed. Breaks. You whisper and splash with ice.
I hug you and brush you. I remove your teeth,

like piano keys, then put them in again. Now you are
different: evolution has leveled the trauma.
They will bite again and flash, they'll rob you
of your sadness. I'll blow you up and pop you again

and again, don't worry, I won't get tired. The skin
needs care and bait. And sometimes you have twelve floors
and we have to figure out immediately if you're a match.

To cut deeper and deeper into your taste. And also: to gently
herd them back, the pedestrians who tumbled out of your wing
at the silliest hour. You are Slovenian, therefore sad.

Translated by Christopher Merrill and the author.

Kiss the Eyes of Peace

Kiss the eyes of Peace, may it stream down
upon the trees. The sun shines and no longer roars
so intolerably. The soul again hopes to sense its
ribs, the sap. The cold has done me good. If the wind
blows, and I walk and watch the cars, life
brings me back to itself. It would be terrible
not to recognize anyone at the departure.
They'd be too far to touch or
be felt. In the pitch darkness I would not hold the memory
of love. A crust of ice forms on molten lava.
In time I might again be able to slide off. Walk
those roads of dust. Shake the jacket off, if it's
dusty. There has been too much honey and grace, that's
all. Too many blessings break a man apart.

Translated by Mia Dintinjana.

Milan Dekleva

There is Still No Name for You

For anything more will we be able to die.
Close by heaven's abyss kneels the last grace.
The stone embraces nakedness, again tries to take it.
Peace is complete to the depth, you can hear the light fall.

You have grown out of the superstition that life goes through everything.
We have looked you through and through and have not recognized you.
With your beauty you entered our marrow, seizing us all.
For you there is still no name: we would fear it all too much.

From their decaying material the patched homes run with tears.
We are theirs, pressing ever closer in brightness.
Our breath becomes harsh and divinely thin.
We dwell heroically in ignorance, like in a school exercise.

Translated by Alasdair MacKinnon.

Anaximander is Measuring

Staring to the stars, as gods used to.
A Greek by profession, charmed by relations,
seven times higher than my own feet,
seven times more silent than my own mouth which has spat out
the tongue found by the Forgotten One
in a small shrub. Staring to the stars.
A Greek by profession. I am realizing that the earth
floats, but not on water, as Thales believed.
I am not naive. I still transplant words
from the earth to the woman's joint, gardening solitude
of the dead: deeper from evil or goodness is
the blue indifference of beauty.

Translated by Boris A. Novak.

Anaximander is Dreaming

A rooster, spy of the light, has taken my head away
and bequeathed it to the river.
A bumblebee, the stepson of the sun, has stung my shoulder
changing it into dew.
A raven, the charcoal purpose of fire, has untied my navel
spilling me into the trembling sky.

I was awake.
A trembling body mourned without a shadow.
In the meantime the river has met the sky in the dew.

Translated by Mia Dintinjana.

The Origin of Language

Women talk the jargon of shattered flowerbeds.
The sick talk from pain.
Stones from stoniness.
The stars mumble the gravitation of light.
To the prophet and illusionist the voice lends revelations.
The meadows are littered with alphabets of ants,
the cantilena of towns is a criss-cross of errands.

Only freedom speaks the patois of its own being,
which is freedom.
That speech is on the boundary.
It convenes the whole world
to the human ear.
Encircles us, as death encircles life.
Like wide-open doors we flap in time,
the hundred times safeguarded secret
of worthlessness.

Translated by Alasdair MacKinnon.

Limping Sonnet

A cypress wanted to be a sonnet,
and words heard her.
An upright poem. Who was her grandfather?
She grew into a pure state. Silenced
by distances of the winds: by them she measured the world.

Into her cobalt branches' growth wove
lovers' glances, murders, quiet misfortunes.
With these, she carelessly straightened
through droughts, tempests, the sun's assaults, the painful
greeting of snows. She gave

uprightness to everything, and thus withstood all.
To the deeds of the good and the evil she added

the sentience of wood. And a cypress cone, a bee sting
of heaven, to carry on with the making of poems.

Translated by Mia Dintinjana.

Milan Jesih

From *Volfram*

Unseen angels walk noiselessly—barefoot without stirring the wind
    around the sleeping houses; this is now.
Wooden I lie awake in *didaskalia*, my eyes weary, mouth dry, with a heart
    that knows everything: everything,
when even nothing was too much. The merciless hour of sheet—the date—
    gone, impressing no memory of its traces.
Just like those angels outside leaving no footprints in the grass. Bread is
    melting in the cupboard.
On chandeliers flies are lulled into a light sleep. I, too: just to fulfill
    the longing of my eyelids! To slide into sleep!

But there are no angels: it is I who unknowingly stumble in blind images
    around neighbors, scenting their wives
and daughters instead of being in my room; let all of me fall asleep,
    rest my eyes and give dreaming wings
to my bubbling blood. The heart knows everything (when even nothing
    was too much), but is still fond of pounding:
perhaps this is the only true way of being. This is now: the cherry branch
    in the vase is locked in a spawning of time;
on the table cooked spinach, made for the noon meal, hovers in water.

        *   *   *

The city quarter of Šentvid is golden—washed by a rainstorm, made
    serene by the sun's brightness,
calmed by a fresh wind from the Gorenjska fields. The soul, likewise,
    longs to rest:
I sit by the window with a sleeping book in my arms, lost in the dark blue
    of the sky, too shy to get up,
tired of sitting, melancholic after reading the lives made into literature.
    Sunk in thoughts: my mother believed

everything was predestined, I've insisted that man chooses for himself and
      therefore

I kept putting off a great deal of time for some future time—and it so
      happened that my present self
and my future self stayed awake for some fat years. Now there is nothing
      promising or encouraging, the heart freed
from the weight of a hopeless hoping: it is time to turn the TV on, foreign
      wars and long legs of sniper guns,
and simply be. To chase the corrosion out of the heart, though—who can
      tell? The air is soft, each breath grace:
Oh, clouds! Lambs that escaped to the sky! Aided by winds, kind brothers,
      they reached the heights of their dreams!

         *   *   *

The night is dark and silent. Only when a shy south wind blows, the open
      window winces and the dancer
in the curtain pleats stirs. The night is a dark solitaire, deep like a grave
      and as gently inviting, softly luring:
it kneads doubt into the heart dough, filling people's bodies with anxiety,
      and they desire to escape out,
across currant bushes and gardens, across streets, bridges and meadows,
      through mountains crushed to scree,
over straits and birch trees—away into a freshly-dug distance;

the evil steals itself into everything, gnawing the skin, corroding metals—
      utter destruction is its measure:
even when for a moment a tiny flame begins to shine in a rat in a cellar or
      an insect in pea blossoms,
a flame that is hope and faith, it hunts it down and kills it. The air in the
      room is humid, scentless,
without memory—its presence a shuddering touch to eyelids. With a
      blanket wrapped around my knees
I sink into an armchair and wish to remain that way, frozen in time.

*   *   *

When a tiger sheds its skin—how vulnerable becomes its flesh!—a blanket
      will embrace me like crust,
harsh, dry, sleep with a face of promise will take me in: when an animal
      sheds its skin, when the air is expansive
on a plain, how full of death the room becomes! Who was I? White
      distances,
savage naked beauty, an intense presence, bubbling miracle, an inspired
      will—thirty years of childhood,
much pathos and milk and—ho!—the terrifying unfulfillment of man!
And so what? Should wars start so I'll pull myself together? and have,
      ashen from fear, one wish only:
to live? Or an unexpected love in Italy. Or snails, slithering in the moist
      garden. Or coal in cellars.
It is not true that the sound of an accordion is heard in times like such.
      Nothing is heard.
Nothing is there. I smell of sweat. My shirt, my wrist-watch and weights.
      No manifestations of change:
everything remains in its assigned, improper place.

*   *   *

I have arrived and it is true: the house has neither the teeth of a sea-urchin
      nor the hopes of wives rebelling
against their husbands: the blossoms of the hallway are opening, the weight
      of rain is foreign, left outside.
Here there is only the good old sameness: the halted thought of an angel
      and traces of the fragrance of hay.
What, then, do I bring: not a gift or letter in my hands, not a heart or star
      inside my chest: just some barefoot words
behind my ear—I put my T-shirt on and between drinking and salvoes,
      without a shade of distance,

I watch spellbound—as if in oblivion, or in devastation, or some different,
      distant life—
a small table made of black rosewood, encrusted with copper, on it three

napkins, three teaspoons,
cocoa in three little cups: oh! the interior so tranquil in a stable charisma
  and enchanted symmetry,
leaving me breathless, opiated, removing past and future lives as the fragile
  rain rustles
behind young curtains like the divination of a prophet.

* * *

At night, when birds are asleep, there are stars the birds don't know
  of unless they open their eyes
from the pain of dreams. Night is a soft discreet charm: luring is the playful
  pliable hour—offering,
but in truth taking, bringing tears smilingly; and how it showered itself
  with flowers! and the gentle wind;
its mane, adorns its nape, spoiled by kisses! and the tempting siren-like
  silence, the night's magic spell
which is killing, killing, killing everything, and iron and the pristine pagan
  faith!

The birds are oblivious to this and to the stars unless they open their eyes
  from the pain of their dreams and stare,
bewildered, into the night. They don't know of me digging ceaselessly
  inside myself to find a memory
that would console me, forgetting I am not a mine. Then, what am I?
  A huge blueberry,
full of sharp human horrors; distance and promise; and the birds don't
  know, the birds are asleep. They know nothing
unless they open their eyes from the pain of their dreams as a cold shiver
  awakens the soft cores of their hearts.

* * *

This unknown village—strewn on the slope as if it wished to climb
  the mountain—his village is my home.
My heart knows its church-bells, its apple-trees in blossom, the old men

and women and their south seas,
their northern fears. It was there I experienced all the big things of my
     childhood: my father's joke,
the clear laughter of my mother, a headless rooster, matches in a hayloft
     and all the things
and thoughts permeated with a healthy ardent anticipation.

Distances, distances. Now I sit in the brittle library of a dark foreign city,
     my blood throbbing lazy and lethargic
in my temples. The village! maidens are rocking their breasts under thin
     linen,
while I have deliberately chosen the bare life, denounced everything to
     quench my thirst for learning, so I'd not stay small
in myself; a pearly honey has gathered around my pain, passions
     evaporate after being stirred
by the forceful winds of time—and afterwards we don't know how it all
     was or what the life was all about.

       *   *   *

Morning, a graceful morning arose amid the mountaintops; no force can
     hold back the fragility of time
in its awakened trepidation; like nothing can hold back the growth of day,
     the opulence of light; and what has rotted
in the heart cannot be brought back to life: all through the night—an
     intense new moon in May—
I was writing a poem: of my heart's desire for joy, affection and truth.
     But, I gave birth to pain:
my poems became a vessel of distress, and the shards of my broken life
     are now staring at me.

The world is asleep, faces peaceful; if not for their likeness to blossoms I'd
     think they were dead.
My fingernails hurt from the lazy passing of minutes, grating my trembling:
     I am a human bomb,
a scream of despair! The forest is oblivious to ants and people: everything

ever coming to life
in it will return from the same into the same. I spread honey on bread,
      milk is boiling,
I take a clean napkin; an immense drop of the sun's light floods the shadows
      of earth.

Translated by Sonja Kravanja.

Boris A. Novak

Uni-verse

The light and its night: shapes and their shades, waves and shores—their
   graves,
and the moon not only full but fulfilled: and a field—a handful
   of distance,
and the wind—a forefinger of the air, and a bird—a wedding ring of nothing:

and a traveler and his traveling toward the end of steps, into the root
of an endless circle: a voice, and yet a silence of everything,
the silence, and yet a praise to everything: wondering blossoms among
   petals of senses:

touch is the nearest neighbor of the untouchable: a secret weaving of birth:
   a native
death: a mystery of word, a word of mystery: universe, a unison of unheard
   star chimes,
universe, an unspeakable rhyme of rhymes, universe, one and only
   cosmic verse...

Translated by Boris A. Novak.

Interior

Mysterious are the characters of things close to us:
familiar as a man's face, but strangely near
from ceaseless use: but between the two
who is a man and who is a garment?

Silent is the tongue of the shoes put on.
(Things that serve are silent.)
When I take them off, they suddenly speak up:
a bottomless abyss since I am no longer there.

When I take off my glasses, what do they see?
Without them I see only myself. Insane.
Things live, I am alive and alone.

I sleep alone in a closet. When I unlock my eyelids,
I see gaping sleeves of my jacket
and my trousers without my legs. Empty.

Translated by Irena Zorko Novak and the author.

Exile

No star can help me any more.
I stare into the frozen northern skies,
the south is hidden. The white city
where I was raised lies
dying beyond the starry wall of the southern horizon.
An ever thicker crust separates
me from myself. And I can only see
the shadow of my dead half through a moist
mist: as if I tremble, having no bottom,
and touch my dark face.
My only home is my throat.

Translated by Andrew Wachtel, Irena Zorko Novak and the author.

Living Shadow

Shadowy ancestor, I seek you everywhere.
I follow you wherever light still glows,
but I lose myself, for I am heir
to your eternally obliterated grave.
Mine is a dim and late epoch:
the mirror is a vanishing well.
But faithfully you accompany me
for you are my living shadow.

I cannot go after you. The anguish
of the past and the weight of the wreath
are more than I can bear. But softness
remains, a miraculous presence.
I freely breathe the flowers from your grave.
I have been relieved from my shadow.

Translated by Irena Zorko Novak and the author.

Meta Kušar

From *Silk and Flax*

Photosynthesis is a legitimate process
taking place between the lips and the look,
between fingers and chalk.
In darkness the reefs are small and elsewhere,
as if they were not in the middle.
Look, the sea!
It is not despair and fear.
The error of the world drives me to tears.

*

Like brittle old underskirts
the wings rustle.
The soul never wakes alone.
Angels come and help,
as at immolation, where they stand arranged
on black, on white tiles and work.
In my cathedral it is the book spines
that are light and dark. It is there
that the blond and the dark congregate.
To change wine into life
or bread into a body
is not the work of one man.

*

He who has not had enough
gets stuck together.
What a burial of culture.
Even more. Ashes of the heart!

Intellectual promiscuity folds tightly,
into a small
twenty-gram tea box.

*

No sign of spring yet.
Ice and wind are stronger
in the sun.
Surrender to suffering quietly.
Without the wrong word.
Angel, who borrows an old, sick, yellow body.

*

Do you know love stories?
History?
Thoughts from the cellar? Secret teachings,
which support the bed just like lotions,
cooking pots and roses on the lookout
for anyone who
might have the key?
In the garden, nerves are immobile,
but I am wondering how he
changed the souls of the living and the dead.

*

No no, the blossom lacks nothing.
On the emerald table lie two laws
which are one.
A keen eye is checking agreements,
connections, causes;
because the less visible world lives so
that it moves what happens here.

*

He is explaining
how all physical changes tend
toward heat.
The laws of nature are discovered?
He knows that love ruins statistics?
He knows the direction of the world behind the house?
He is small enough to circle on his own.
In my memory,
cascades of lilac blossoms over white richelieu.
Little silver spoon, *oeufs farcis en variétés.*
Fettine al burro profumato.
Scampi all aglio.
Ludvik is bashing *zabaglione.*
Oh! What a memory!
Champagne!
Not this one!
This begging is madness.

*

In a kiss there is something
that fails to make the beaten silver of the moon disappear.
Only yellow scents of the island
remain on the edges of winter,
folded in like this.

*

What is gathering on papers? On the soles of feet?
Do you register the shine as it leaves the soul?
Is this destiny?
Nerves suffer under the weight of arguments.
I know you didn't tear the precious tissue.
You overlooked a few signs of soul happiness.

There are still things that tremble.
Again and again day turns out to be more than time.
Agates are sending me
across the water, while the oracles demand
gentle service.
Running, I tear the veil.
How tattered it is.
This line in the palm of my hand.

Translated by Evald Flisar.

Majda Kne

Hasanaginica

I'll howl at the train in the full moon and in no moon,
and footsteps will be heard down the hallway. the day
will be sunny, hoar-frost on trees and grass. in the old town
by the river I choose a window someone lives behind. he is
not home, there is no light. I am learning to sit alone
and let the film keep rolling. a journey around the world
becomes condensed into a dot. it is a long journey.
that, however, never interrupts their dance. make no conversation
on the street, hide into the night. place your hands next
to your body, let the dust gather and the room become impassable.

Quadruple Voices: Quadrophenia

a trembling poplar grew,
I graze the greenery in my village.

a joyful exchange:
to graze on trees as tall as the third floor,
to compose magnificent trunks for daisies.

a silent swamp ghost
has risen from the rotten green fog.

Strung Seeds

when someone walks on rotten snow,
is judged by swamps,
sits on the window sill and watches people
traveling across the world—
these are maidens
that need to be rebuilt.

it is a pallid day for slaying children,
one waits night and morning for joyous times.

Barefoot March

a small million words have been said about your
springtime, inhabited by loud music. a dog barks
after you and when you look at it I see a face.
repetition: a few letters and my inability to,
whenever I come, leave the house for the field
or the village green. streets resonate from three
sides, and from the fourth a brook clatters under
a graveyard. as one jumps over it there is a road
behind the plain, leading to a small town. they'll
look at me with suspicious curiosity. in the middle
there is a church, visible from the entire plain.
we stand on the white sun, I see things fleetingly,
though standing there is longer than time. a poet,
a woman; as I watch them I see myself watching.
there is a recognition between us, and a contemptuous
silence. we are, quite possibly, also dead. like the
sky, dropping bombs silently; blue smoke rises gently,
slowly, from the green grass. in the hotel's windows
are contorted images of magnificent buildings. scenes
from before-death, falling of the body, riddled by sword-stabs.
a faun dozes, wakes up, dozes and wakes up among the
white swamp flowers. I grab this dark image of mine.

Translated by Sonja Kravanja.

Maja Haderlap

Nothing Remains

nothing remains of the illusion of security, which settles like a sickness
in the memory and persists, impatient. here the endless knot, so that i am at
     a loss for words;
for years and years the elevator descends to a hallway too low and the
     vineyards outside
recall the place. impermanence has seized the walls, the innuendoes.

total alarm veils the audacious charm: anew i choose among the phantoms
     of home
and abroad, and attempts at domestication come to naught in flight. i note
     the ancient grievance
and the idea of the experience of weakness, as if it could not increase,
and remembrance is shortened into the fleeting sensation that makes the
     microbes tremble.

My Cautious Coming

my cautious coming into the world forces me into embarrassment, no longer
        can i
bewitch despair with a gentle thought, no longer do i try to eradicate what
        has happened
in my head. the end awaits immensely, and nonchalant movements in the
makeshift
dwelling-place here erase the impressions. i am sober as never before.

and what i said will need completing. all the visible and previous days have
        gathered
in a motley cumulus and what have i not sketched with glances into the single
        significance
of time with the idea of happiness! o, final irresponsibility, neither
        deceiving
nor corrupting. the watery mosaics are surging everywhere. i am entering, i
        enter.

There Are Days

there are days when tapestries are hanging in the town for the curious
      japanese
and platinum lights shimmer like silver over the entrances. there is a time
      when memory
comes from the promised land quite absently and deceptively, and death is
      cool only
when touched. the day is all jagged, trampled, and there is no plea for life.

there are cramped times when i choose incarnate stupidities anywhere, i
      approach on tiptoe,
i swallow them and would just believe all of it: the singing, the sentence
which deserves to be reconciled a bit later and becomes numb with repetition.
      sensuous is
the god whom i have wooed and who, with opium lips, makes fun of the
      orphan, of anyone.

Translated by Tom Priestly.

Aleš Debeljak

Elegies from the North I

Earth. Red earth. And tall grass as far as you can see. You're pressed to the ground. Hidden from unwanted glances. Utterly still. A quail by your ear. Are you turning into stone? No: you're just listening to shadows fall over cornfields. A bead of sweat—a tear?—slides down your cheek. In the distance a mountain rises steeply. Naked. Without trees or flowers. Imprinted on the sharp-edged horizon. On its peak, lost in the clouds, generations of stag hunters wander for centuries. Glistening of the setting sun. All the signs say: end of Indian summer. If I hear it right, nothing comes from your lips. Are you dumb? Blind? Perhaps you're searching through memory for the shapes of all prints—footsteps in the snow, old songs and cognac in the evening, small white towns with castles and turrets, the smells of Sunday afternoons, the river running under granite bridges. As if this, too, escapes you. Here, under the empty sky of ancient tribes you never heard about, you'll end your way. I, of course, always return. You don't. Which makes all the difference.

Elegies from the North II

The sodden moss sinks underfoot when we cross half-frozen bays and walk through birch groves, wandering in an uneven circle that widens into darkness, through the minds and bodies of men and animals trapped in last year's snow—no: trapped from the beginning, emptiness all around us, ice collecting on our pale faces, I can hear you singing on the run, an unknown melody, I can't make out the words, clouds of breath freeze on your fur collar, eyes open wide as we trudge through silence and weakening starlight, through the fevered babble of children exiled to distant camps, insects curling up under bark, December or June, no difference, ashes blanket the ground as far as you can see, damp wool of shirts, we wade through the fog rolling in from the hills, oozing into our lungs, hills where there must be flowers about to bloom under a woman's eyelids, who dreams of dark faces hardening into granite, the snow's covering us, we're asleep on our feet, under the steel-gray sky, oblivious to the rhythms of sunrise and sunset, endless, as if they never began, our teeth crack in the cold, we don't want to separate, I can barely swallow, tell me the lyrics of your song, I want to sing with you.

Elegies from the North V

Now, in a bitter or a soft voice, in the lengthened melodies of a lament, in flooding and cracked mirrors, brute force of soldiers and the blind offspring of nomadic animals disturb your sense of reality, which changes like shifting archipelagos in the South Seas, now, in lush cascades of corn, flowing toward a sewer like the pale blood of mortally-wounded dolphins, in moments of horror, before you sink into sleep, which won't release you from the memory of exile, now, when you say *snow* and everything remains the same, in a sad song, slyly imitating the rhythm of a long run across infinity, now, hopelessly, passionately, hastily here, the door ajar, through which water leaks, now, when the walls are closing in and snail shells crack underfoot, now, in the ripe clusters of hail nailing you to the ground, now, at the end and beginning of paths closing, now, in the dark voice coming from the night you shared with everyone lost like you: do you recognize yourself in this poem?

Late Evening Light VII

Another beginning: it doesn't make any sense. I'd rather not even try again. And yet: this image, this faded photograph of you, your sad face, your hands on your lap (do I only imagine it?), in a room with friends—yet not altogether there. The photograph is still here. Along with all the things you wanted then. You know exactly what you believe! How to spend the night, when to bare your shoulders. How carefully you choose your words, which sound so perfect! You talk today, whenever, with anyone. What happened doesn't change anything. The children at your feet play with dominoes made from the bones of animals. Closets filled with smoked glass. Perhaps a book or two. Open on the shelf. Now you can tell me what you kept for years from the ones closest to you. The future's already here. Tell me everything. Ups and downs, the habits of your heart, silences, mild mornings, long-distance calls, sighs, whispers, hopes, fears. I'm no longer here for you to hurt. The gust of autumn wind in the chimes clinking on the balcony: only you can hear it.

A River and a Young Woman V

After all, why sadness? Why fear? We don't know the depths of Finnish lakes, the cold of the Siberian taiga, the map of the Gobi desert. We don't even know what's in your dreams. Mine, too. That's the way it is. But you, as always: listening in the dark, lighting matches, gazing straight ahead. The man whose name you won't forget—even in the middle of the night—still hasn't called. You're hungry. In the corner of the room an old man in a rocking chair creaks back and forth, the shining keys of the sax laid on its side reflect your soft face, which you hide from yourself and others. Framed by the window, horses hover above the ground, wandering aimlessly through men's destinies, silk tails sailing in the wind. And for a moment, while the old man leans over a book—leafed through hundreds of times—you see the riders galloping across the fields, through the woods, heads down, black hair waving in the setting sun, the vanishing sun. Gone. Is that why you can't remember the short poem describing the whole world as it was and will be, why dusk blinds you to the stories of everyone, stories known only to the man whose name you won't forget—even in the middle of the night, the man who stands somewhere in the open, alone, on the high plains?

Ways of Saying Goodbye VI

The river rushes on. As it has for a long time. Herons, or wading birds that look like the herons in field guides, are getting ready to fly south. Reeds rustle in the evening wind, in the breeze off the water. Here and there. The houses lining the bank fade in mist. Pale light fills the windows. Seated by the lamps, people dream of soldiers entering their lives. Sweet apples in their cellars: if no one eats them, they'll begin to rot. A thirteen-year-old girl keeps practicing piano sonatas. Stiff fingers. Steady wind. Hours running on. In everyone's eyes: growing boredom. Think twice. You can also bid farewell. After all, you'll only be changing ways of saying goodbye. I was just like you long ago.

Empty Rooms V

The dripping tap. Keepsakes in the drawer. Glowing coals. The cat's nest on a friend's bed. The sky comes down. Fruit rots in the grass. Bruised by September. Abstracted, you stroll down the back streets, through the coastal village. The port drifts off to sleep, moaning in terror. In bare feet you feel the earth, every stone, every plant. Time, unspent, hardens in the bronze bells of the cathedral. Another strange sound, like the sigh of a sick child in early evening, vanishes into nothingness, into history. Are you coming? Going? Your hand's half-raised to greet or wave goodbye, like this:

Translated by Christopher Merrill and the author.

Fiction

An excerpt from
A Day in Spring

Ciril Kosmač

It was a lovely day in spring, full of light and sound, as if cast in pure silver.

It is true that at times the dark clouds of a tragic past drifted across the clear sky of my memories; it is true that griefs, old and recent, often beat upon the sullen walls of my heart; it is true that former impetuous emotions of youth would sometimes rise again to the surface; it is true that in the depths of the cold pool of life's actuality, the heavy stones of drowned longings would stir and, sighing, turn again; but all this could not overshadow, or trample, or undermine, or break up the broad meadow of my peace. Oh no! All the passions that, untamed and unsatisfied, still raged in the dark recesses of my being, could not erode the precious soil deposited there, layer by layer, by the river of five-and-thirty years of sharp experience, most of it troubled and stormy. So then, this day in spring was truly lovely, full of light and sound, as if cast in pure silver.

And just so was Kadetka who, all unexpectedly, came with it.

To begin with, I woke up long before dawn, in the middle of the night. This was not strange in those days in May at the end of the War. At that time, every evening found me housed in a different part of the country, and every morning summoned me from a light sleep to new decisive events which drew me forth at once upon the road and carried me away with bewildering speed from Črnomelj to Ravna Gora, from Ravna Gora to Ajdovščina, to Trieste, Gorizia, and finally along the graygreen waters of our Soča to my native Tolmin home. I slept lightly and uneasily. Every sound was like a blow in my ears, forever on the watch at night, and always I would start up and open my eyes, weary yet alert, and longing for the sight of home surroundings and familiar faces.

And now, too, I jerked my head upright and looked about me. I was lying in a low-ceilinged, narrow loft flooded with soft moonlight which filtered in through a single window, barred and screened. I stared in wonder, but only for a moment, because even before I had asked myself where I was, I recognized the loft, the window and the moonlight. I smiled, and the blissful thought which flashed up in me even before the smile pressed me back upon my pillow like a kind, familiar hand. I closed my eyes, but my heart and all my body was thrilled by a sense of calm and perfect happiness so strong that I had to tell myself, aloud: "I am at home! After fifteen years I am in bed once more under my own roof!"

I lay down and greedily inhaled the air. It was soft, close, and pleasantly cool, like the dark wines of my country. At once I felt a new and heady vitality in my veins. Lightheartedly, I clasped my hands behind my head and abandoned myself to the undulating murmur of that spring night. It rocked me as in a cradle and began to raise me up and up. Soon it bore me to such heights of ecstasy that, with all the fervor of the boy within me, I began to recite under my breath:

> Dear home of my birth, oh house of my father's roof,
> The poor man's castle, goal of the wand'rer afar;
> The dove beneath foreign skies, bent on her homeward flight
> Has longing to show her the way and guide her aright...

The words sounded rich and solemn as would the anthem of a downtrodden people raised freely after a profound silence of centuries. The resonance of them expanded my chest and quickened my heartbeat. But oh! as suddenly my heart gave back a bitter ache, so poignant and overpowering that it hurled me down from my clouds of soaring rapture.

"That's how it is!" I sighed. "Longing showed me the way through all those restless years. I have found the goal... And what have I found?"

The bitter truth loomed up before me like a rugged, perpendicular cliff.

And in an instant I had run into it. My happiness that had been so calm and pure was broken up and troubled. Again the poem spoke. The words were still resonant and solemn, but they sounded grim and bitter:

> Dazed, the doves are circling above the burning house...
> Forlorn my thoughts lament my desolate native land...
> A gray day dawns: we are scattered far and wide,
> As the needs of life compelled, or the unrest in our hearts;
> Only the swallows remain in their shelter under the eaves—
> We are stricken by the storm that has whirled us afar...

Slowly the poem was engulfed in my bitter and angry mood. Yes, all that the poet said was true, all, only nowhere was there safe shelter! No, there was none, not even in this remote and lonely cottage! Like a monstrous, red-hot steam roller, the war had passed over the length and breadth of our land, crushing everything, scattering everything, ourselves included. There had been seven of us under this roof, and now I had come home and found just one single swallow: only our little Auntie is at home, taking care of this three-hundred-year-old nest and waiting for the birds to come back. If they do come back. My brother and sisters are sure to do so, because I know that they are alive, but my Father will never return. He waited and waited, the old diehard, and even survived till this spring. Barely a month ago, the last winter winds scattered his ashes over German soil. Auntie doesn't know yet. From the first day of the Liberation, she has been airing his Sunday blacks, which greeted me yesterday so grimly from the blossoming branches of our old pear-tree that I stood as if turned to stone.

I shook my head to drive away the memory of it, but it refused to leave. I saw myself quite plainly, rounding the corner and coming to a halt in the middle of the yard. Auntie stopped too, but only for a moment. Then she recognized me and flew up to me with a cry of joy such as I had never before heard from her lips. She pressed both my hands, sobbed, and brokenly told me all that needed to be told. Then she dried her eyes with her apron and with her skinny fingers pushed a wisp of gray hair back under her faded black kerchief. Her keen eyes took stock of the whole of me, she nodded cheerily, and said with a happy sigh, "Oh dear, how pleased your father will be!"

I looked at the clothes, so like a black banner waving idly in the spring breeze. Auntie followed my eyes, smiled and said with gleeful pride, "Yes, they're his. For two years I had them hidden. In the bedroom, and the corn-bin, in the byre and the hayloft, in the henhouse and the pigsty, shifting them from one hiding place to another... Oh, don't look at me like that. You'll never guess why I hid them so carefully"

I shook my head.

"Just think how heartless people have grown," Auntie cried angrily and clenched her fists. "No, you wouldn't believe it, but the very same evening they marched your father off, Martin-Beyond-the-Dam came shambling up to the house, spat a mouthful of brown slime, and said quite coolly, 'Annie, I've come for Andrew's duds.' And then he spat again. It's true that Martin hasn't heart enough for half a man; it's true that he's been a gravedigger these thirty years, but all the same his words went through me like a knife. You can imagine I didn't find an answer at once. But Martin just went on, and this time he hurt me still more. 'He'll surely never put them on again himself,' he yapped and waved his hand. It froze me to the marrow of my bones, but I got back my breath. 'Well then, you won't either!' said I—I was just boiling inside. It doesn't sound nice, but I tell you straight, if I'd had a knife in my hand, I'd have gone for him with it. But, because I hadn't, I just hissed at him, 'You dead man's croaker, have you taken to burying folks alive?' Martin looked at me from under his brow, spat, and then he said, cold as ice, 'Over there they do bury them alive... In fact I'm told they never bury them at all. Too many of 'em. I'm told they just burn 'em up in ovens.' I felt so wild with rage that I was more than a match for him. 'Then I'll light the stove myself and burn his things. After all, I've got plenty of wood in the house.'"

Auntie heaved a great sigh of relief and then pushed back that rebellious strand of hair which had once more escaped from under the kerchief and looked at me brightly as if to say, "Didn't I tell him off properly?"

"You told him off properly." The words almost choked me.

"All right," she proudly agreed. "He took himself off. But when he was out of the cowshed I began to tremble. I hid all of your father's things which were still of some value. These blacks of which he was so proud I shifted from one place to another, yet I was always afraid for them. Three times a day I would go and look whether they were still where I had hidden them, and do you know why? Oh, you'll never believe me. You'll tell me that I'm an old fool. Yes, do, because I really am! Just think, the very first night it suddenly came to me in a dream: 'Martin's a gravedigger. Isn't that a sign that father won't come back anymore?' I shivered and stared into the dark.

But then something whispered to me: 'If you keep his clothes he'll come back; if you lose them he won't.' Of course I realized at once that that was just an old wife's foolishness. But I felt better. You don't know how I clung to this thought. I just drew myself up. And when I met Martin I made fun of him in my mind and shook my finger as if I would make fun of death and shake my finger at it: 'Oh, no, you don't!'"

My eyes were fixed on her long and slightly crooked bony finger, which seemed almost transparent in the evening sun. Then I looked her in the eyes. Their expression was a mixture of frank surprise and veiled pride. She was obviously waiting for a word from me. And as no word came, she passed her hand over her forehead with that familiar gesture, although that lively wisp of hair was scarcely showing from under the kerchief. She shook her head and sighed. "An odd thing, isn't it? What I want to say, isn't it odd that one gets obsessed with such thoughts. After all the horrors we've been through, it's silly, isn't it?"

"We don't know yet what we've been through." I slowly wrung the words out of my throat.

"Oh, what we know is quite enough!" Auntie made a resolute gesture and again wiped her forehead.

"But I ask you, are such thoughts silly or not? Tell me straight!"

"Of course they're silly," I agreed miserably.

"They've got such a tight hold on me! But don't think the worse of me for that! An old body may get slack about faith, but she'll never shake off superstition!"

"That's probably true," I said.

"Of course it's true," nodded Auntie. "Well, now I've done at least with that superstition."

She waved her hand and went to the clothes. She straightened a sleeve which the wind had lifted and entangled with the wild shoots of the dying tree. Then she nodded happily and called out: "Just think how glad he'll be! He'll come home straight from the camp, all dirty and in rags. God knows where they've dragged him about, poor dear, and where he's tramping now! Well, he'll have a wash and change. You know yourself that he always liked to be well dressed."

"I know, I know," I murmured.

"Do you remember, when he'd changed on Sunday afternoon, how he used to pace the room with his head thrown back? He'd turn on his heel ever so lightly, shake his shoulders and look at himself. Mother would give a little laugh and then clap her hands and admire him out loud: 'My, how handsome you are!' But he stood still, drew himself up even more, stroked the bridge of his nose with his open hand and agreed quite seriously, 'Of course I'm handsome!' Do you remember how they both used to laugh then?"

"I know, I know," I murmured rather more loudly, resolutely lifting my feet and turning toward the threshold.

"And mother would laugh at him even now if she were alive," continued Auntie as she followed me. "And she would laugh at you, because you, too, like to show off your new clothes. Do you remember how she used to clasp her hands and say to your father, 'Oh, but that boy takes altogether after you! Just look at him! As if born to be a lord!' Father would laugh, and then say very seriously, 'Nancy, we'll both be glad if it turns out that he's not born to be a slave!' And he was right, wasn't he?"

Without a word I crossed the threshold. Auntie followed me. The big room was all washed and scrubbed and tidied as if on the eve of a holiday. All four windows were wide open, but I noticed the fumes of petrol all the same.

"Isn't there a smell of petrol?" I asked.

"Of course there is," Auntie nodded, well pleased with herself.

"I've cleaned and oiled the harmonium. You know that he'll sit down to it at once and try to get some music out of it. He was always very much taken up with it, especially these last years. Not even in our worst straits would he think of parting with it. And you may believe me that we were really in straits if I tell you that he would get up in the middle of the night and begin playing in the dark. But why am I telling you all this when you remember it yourself! The cows went from the shed, the larches from the meadow, there's not a walnut tree left beside the house, nor an oak, but the harmonium is still here. I can't quite understand that. You know, I've no ear for music."

I nodded and fixed my eyes on the harmonium, which stood behind the door all bright with polish. The lid was open. The light played upon the black and white keys as if they were alive and waiting impatiently for the touch of a hand.

"Do you remember," resumed Auntie after a silence, "how your father would say that some people have hearts even though they've got no ear?"

"I know," I nodded and looked at her.

"He used to say it about me, too," she said slowly. She pushed that rebellious strand of hair from her forehead and gave me a lively glance.

"I don't remember," I lied.

"It's all the same," she waved a deprecating hand. "This war has been such a thunderstorm that even I haven't escaped the lightning. I hope that it opened my heart and that now I can hear."

"I hope so, too," I smiled at her.

She opened her arms and pointed around the room. "You see I've got everything ready," she boasted. "I've thought of everything!"

"I see," I agreed.

She laughed happily. Suddenly she opened her mouth, clutched her head with both her hands and looked at me with something like horror. "But I forgot about you!" she cried. "Good Lord, I'm looking at you as if you were a stranger. You must be hungry! And where are you going to sleep?"

I tried to laugh it off. "Well, I really am something of a stranger! I'm not hungry, and I'll sleep in my loft if the old bedstead is still there."

"It is, it is! I'll first go and make your bed and then you'll have supper," said Auntie resolutely and whirled out of the room.

I went up to the harmonium, drew my fingers over the cold, dumb keys and then slowly closed the lid. I turned and paced the room. I patted the backs of our ramshackle chairs and stroked the smooth, worm-eaten table. I stood motionless. I felt the old, potent, irresistible peace of home slowly enfolding me again.

Something creaked behind my back. My ear recognized the sound at once. I turned and stared at the old wall clock beside the stove. The poor old thing was hoarsely preparing to strike. It was tilted a little like some nice old woman with her head a bit to one side. After each stroke it trembled slightly, but the stroke was clear and full. The faded round dial looked at me devotedly and nodded meekly as if to say, "Have you forgotten me? You see I'm still here, still alive and still marking time for you."

"Time..." I murmured and strode up to the clock. I lovingly took hold of its face with both hands and put it straight. Immediately the pendulum slowed down and presently stopped.

At that moment tiny footsteps came tripping down the stairs. Auntie opened the door, stood still and gasped, "No, no, just tilt it; its heart is giving out."

"Its heart is giving out?"

"Of course. It's a hundred years old!"

"A hundred years..." I repeated, tilting the clock again and restarting the pendulum.

"That's right," said Auntie, pleased as the regular tick-tock started once more. "Now, do put down your gun and come with me into the kitchen and have something to eat!"

I deposited my knapsack and Sten gun on the seat beside the stove and went into the kitchen. In next to no time, Auntie served me fried eggs and milk. I didn't feel like eating, but I ate because Auntie stood over me, watching me ecstatically as if I were performing some uncommon rite. When I put down my fork, she spun round again briskly. "Good Lord, it's dark already!" she cried and darted out for Father's clothes. She quickly cleared the table and prepared to iron them. "You see, I'll press them tonight," she said. "And not only the trousers, also the coat. I know that he won't be here tomorrow, but all the same, won't it be nice if everything is prepared?"

"Of course it will," I agreed and turned quickly toward the darkened entry.

"Where are you going?" Auntie fussed after me.

"I'm tired," I protested. "We've had little sleep these days."

"Silly old fool that I am. How is it I never thought of that?" Auntie struck her forehead with the flat of her hand. "Of course you've had little sleep! Now go and lie down. Lie down and go to sleep!"

"I will."

I staggered up the steep creaking steps to my loft and lay down. And I actually dropped off quite quickly.

Translated by Fanny Copeland.

An excerpt from
Minuet for the Guitar

Vitomil Zupan

Meta was the name of the girl I was dancing with, putting on a show for Anton, an enthusiastic and encouraging spectator. Meta, by the way, means 'target' in Serbian. The peasants told us they had been out since dawn, burying the dead. The newborn infant was bawling with all the power of his lungs. When the old fellow in the battered hat gave us a loud and lively polka on his squeeze-box, the windowpanes rattled in their frames.

Somewhere near this place, a well-known author had passed away. In the war diary of a certain soldier, I had found the following sentence: "We forget the battles, since they are so much like each other, but we remember the eating, drinking, the music, the women we knew in between."

Life is fine, great, of infinite variety; it is at its best, greatest, most infinite when crammed into one thrilling moment. It is not good for a man to be on his own. Appetite grows with eating. Nothing lasts for ever but there are moments when we taste eternity. Tra-la-la, tra-la-la, carnival's coming, last year I'd nought to do, this year I'm busy. I cannot really say the first sight of Meta delighted me, and when she first took the floor with me, I did not find her very attractive. She was not one of those women who spear your guts with a glance. She needed to be thawed, warmed, given an extra injection of vitality, spurred on to idle fancies, kneaded, shaken, turned into pure sound, and rhythm, strummed on with the fingertips. In the meantime, I would myself undergo a change. Anton believed in me. I had to live for the sake of all those who now lived on in me. I have eaten your flesh and drunk your blood. And you have eaten my flesh and drunk my blood. The ancient Egyptians believed that each man has a double walking the earth. It is perfectly true. My double is stamping his heels on this solid farmhouse floor. He is telling Meta things she has never heard before and will never hear again.

Anton's double was there too, watching, with great joy, the transformation which was taking place among these people in that festive uproar, with everyone happy that the celebration of Miha's arrival in the world was such a great success. Afterwards, we had something to eat and drink, talked in loud voices, sang, then danced once more. My double, the devil of a fellow, soon had a toothless old lady doubled up with laughter; she pressed her palm to her mouth but could not smother her giggles. A careful exploration of Meta's body with fingernails and fingertips revealed that she was wearing only a slip beneath her dress. Black down-at-heel shoes went well with her sturdy limbs. I was surprised at her quick response to my advances, but women always have a seventh sense. She ought to have realized I was only joking, but how could she guess that the whole show was put on for Anton's benefit. She looked fat but her flesh was firm, young, tight. She was one of the women the painter had in mind when he observed that the best models sometimes look like sluts when they are fully dressed. Anyway, just imagine the Venus de Milo in a suburban lady's Sunday best, or picture those Rubenesque beauties wearing folk costume. Their beauty lies in the hip line, in the curve from waist down to knee, in the motion of their rounded buttocks, in the glowing tips of their breasts, in the dimples around the navel, in the mysterious shifting of their thighs, in the frame of the shoulders, in the line that runs down from the nape of the neck to the parting of the ways at the base of the spine. What generous largesse! What bold exposure! The flesh glows with an inner magic. The skin beguiles and every detail offers something more, something more. But it cannot all be taken in at once and breaks up into parts, parts which fuse again into a new whole, and all is in continual motion, ebbing and flowing in changing patterns.

Meta's hair smells of the open country. Her perspiration excites me. Her eyes cloud over and clear again. She would like to plant her teeth in my flesh. Pity she has rough hands; love is not her vocation. Come on, let me kiss your ear. Why are you squealing? Life is not reality; reality admits no daydreams, no ghosts. There are two roads from your knee; that one goes down, down, and disappears, the other climbs up and up, a warm and smooth path to nirvana. But resist me, put up a good fight in our life and death struggle which will leave us both victors, both vanquished. Most intriguing is that hollow below your knee, a mere detail, and yet there is something marvelous about it, something no one has yet defined. When women still had to keep their knees covered and carefully hidden, that point just below the knee was the first stage on the road to paradise. The ancient Greek sculptors hewed such women in stone, beautiful, cold, of finest stock. I was once in a certain art gallery when they started to put the lights on. Walking round a marble figure, I suddenly noticed the hollows below her knees. For a split second, while the lights were coming on, I half-closed my eyes; the stone came alive and I felt the sudden warmth of the Mediterranean sun on my skin and flesh. I just had to embrace her. Why on earth did I do it? I felt like her, both dead and alive at the same time.

Anton's eyes were now glowing like a cat's in the dark. The best of it was that, although I wanted to live for him, I was now so carried away I was thinking only of myself. Some people in this world have families, build houses, buy plots of land, cultivate gardens, sink wells, breed domestic animals, and so on. Others like collecting mushrooms. Still others rule their fellows, wage wars. Some cure the sick, others plan hold-ups. But I have been walking and walking, until at last I have reached here and found my destination, and I have no intention of stirring from here, since a man cannot travel on after he reaches his goal, or can he? You are Meta, the target, the goal. Like an arrow, shot from an unseen, distant bow, I have landed head-first, plumb in the center of the black and white rings, your black and white rings, the rings of your skin, your tresses, your teeth, limbs, your hair, your breasts, your laughter, your screams.

"You two will be getting hitched," said the accordion player. Yes, Anton and I will marry Meta. Kiss Anton, Meta. He is part of me and I am part of him. Kiss him here, by his bandage. Anton smells of Spanish guitars, Anton is a minuet for guitar. Let's drink from two glasses! Three mouths and two glasses in four-four time; play on, accordion, but play the accompaniment, not the melody. Listen, old chap, it goes like this...Tram-ta-ta-tam...ta-ta... Got it? Right, play. We'll all play. We're all taut as bow-strings in the air of the valleys. Here is the first stage on the road to paradise. Paradise is surrounded by a high wall with no gates. You need to know how to get in. And no one can tell you how. Just think, Adolf said, "Make this land German for me." The English say he's a queer, but he isn't. He's a globe-shagger, he loves every square inch of this planet. The English are queers. They don't believe in paradise. They believe only in the Empire. Paradise will remain, the Empire will fall. The Big Three have decided that after the war they will hunt down war criminals. Great sport for them. We shall be looking for those gates to paradise. You draw close, you're almost there, but rough hands reject you, and once again you're spinning through the endless void. Why the panic? Sure we're at attention. What better moment? This is the only banner raised on the road to paradise, a blind and cunning device. This year, we have managed to survive all the seasons, spring, summer, autumn and winter, and now we have the fifth season, meant for those who have no trees to prune, no houses with roofs to repair, but only a night of dreams. You must shed your burdens on the road to paradise; only when you have nothing can you scale the walls of paradise. Throw it all away. Property is bondage. Power is misery. A crown is a hat it rains on, said Frederick the Great. Glory is froth. Dress is the invention of ugly people. Fate is an idea of cowards. Money was invented by thieves who could not remove cities. That almond cake is super. Why don't you want to take your shoes off? The war is over. Can you hear the Alps breathing in the center of Europe? The poacher again sets off to hunt the chamois. He smears his face with soot, so the gamekeeper won't spot him. The Negro smears his face with chalk. Now we're going to have a quite different dance, my darling. We're going to dance the minuet. Soon, you'll see the grace of those noble movements and gentle steps. No one can say what he knows, no one can say what is lurking in him, waiting for a chance to get out. We're not going to live like vegetables, like rotten potatoes, oh no! We're going to live the life of a river wave, a wave that races into the distance and at the same time remains in place, for it's all the same whether wave or river moves on; all is both here and at the same time in the boundless distance. No one has the right to take that thought from me. Masterly, is it not, Anton? My double walks about a German concentration camp with shaven skull and downcast eyes; they beat him, kick him, but he feels no pain, for he has nothing to say. But he knows it all, sees it all and will remember. The last flicker of resistance in the prisoner's spirit must be doused, the camp psychologist instructs the jailers. He must crawl like a dog on all fours, bark and wag his tail, all to order. And how well that cuckoo trick came off. They had to climb up a tree and call out, "Cuckoo, cuckoo!" all day long. All is both here and at the same time in the boundless distance. No one can seize my thoughts with his hand. But I can grab you, Meta. Go on, scream! And scream again! All is both here and at the same time in the boundless distance.

All is here and at the same time in the boundless distance.

Anton and I got up while the rest of them were still asleep. We quietly set off up the road, while the morning mist still lay on the empty grassy slopes and the trees. In such a dawn, a man is far removed from and untrue to himself. What had risen from sleep and trod the hard boards was a mere robot called Berk. Nothing is happening and there is no existence. I think I know why religious people say their morning prayers. In the same way, a wise driver warms up the engine before taking to the road. In spite of everything, I must think, feel, survey the countryside, know that I am alive. The dead of the past few days have not yet started to decompose. I shall remember the new arrival, Miha, for the next ten or twelve years. Eat and crap, Miha. Does anyone know when the morning begins? This morning presumably began at dawn. Or did it?

We arrived at the village when the first sunlight was beginning to break through the mist. The hens were already scrabbling in the yard of the modest homestead. The mules were standing by with drooping heads. How could so many have survived the retreat? A horse already saddled. The early morning bustle of partisans in and out of the houses. A child, apparently male, in a heel-length night-shirt. A sheaf of straw. Doves. A hen with her brood of chickens. A lad with a machine-gun. A peasant woman with a pail of water. For God's sake! Is it going to begin again? Anything you like, but no repetition of the things we already know, please. A cock on a rooftop. How did he get up there? He stretches his neck and crows. This must be the beginning of a new day. Where is the assembly point? Fine, thanks a lot. Maybe, sometime after the war, I shall be walking up and down the terrace of a strange house, without belonging to any organization, without having to remember where I am to report, without wondering where I am going to be posted. Maybe. We reported, then went to a hay-shed, where we bedded down on a heap of hay, first arranging a comfortable depression and a pillow, then gazing up at the underside of the timbers of the loft. The roof tiles were loose in places and the sun shone in through the fissures. Dare we doze off? Hunger would waken us. Our only worry was that we might miss cook-house call. Or maybe it was not so important; after all, we knew potato and maize flour was to be had from the houses, perhaps even milk and bacon, too. "*Nel mezzo del cammin di nostra vita...*"— at the halfway point of our life's road: the opening phrase of Dante's *Divine Comedy*. Thirty years of age, they say it means. By the lines on my palms I estimate I still have long to live. God knows where and how I shall spend my thirtieth birthday. *"Mi ritrovai per una selva occura..."*—I found myself in a dark forest... And I am falling into the abyss, into the depths of the void. But why have I also a pain in the guts? I listen to the dull echo of an inner question: what, at that moment, caused me such pain? I thought of that long, long road before me. I would be always groping for the meaning of things, always deceived, always having a feeling that I could not put into words, that I could never tell others of: I exist, I am, but I do not know why, how or wherefore; I do not know from whence I came nor whither I am bound; I do not know what rules my bodily organs; I cannot imagine why I am sometimes depressed and sometimes full of enthusiasm; I do not even know what lies beneath the soles of my feet. A planet? Minerals? There are a thousand answers—and none. I rose from the abyss with all my nerves jangling. Slowly I calmed down and possibly even dozed off.

Next day, Anton and I parted for a year and some months. We met again on the morning of the day he died.

Toward evening, we attended a meeting and afterwards had a drink in a farmer's house with four ideologists.

Everything was going smoothly and no one felt like hurrying. The faint light of the sunset forecast worse weather to come. When Anton and I took our seats at the meeting, I still did not know I had a twenty-eight hour journey through the rain in front of me.

A meeting is a good way to boost the morale of civilians and troops and also serves to bring together both partners in the struggle and weld them into one whole. A partisan army cannot operate without the close cooperation of the local population. The chief speaker was the commissar, Dolnichar, a schoolmaster by profession. After his speech he sat next to us. We sipped brandy from our flask and smoked Dolnichar's cigarettes. While it was still light, large clouds began to drift across the sky, while down below there were occasional gusts of wind that tossed the curtains on the makeshift stage. The small village, half demolished, was crammed with people. Ages ago, settlers from the valley had taken refuge here and built their homes. In the paradise to come, their descendants would go down again into the valley. A hundred years back, a hundred years on—what did this day mean to me? I seemed to be floating in a timeless vacuum. Not so long since, there had been a lake in the Ljubljana basin, and at its edge the lake-dwellers had their huts on piles driven into the mud. Then the lake receded and Maria Theresa started to drain the moorland. And I could now see what that plain would look like tomorrow or the day after, with no difficulty. I could see and realize what had been and what was to be. It was harder for me to grasp what was happening at that precise moment. Incidents, sensations, scenes, words—all fused into a steady, simultaneous ebb and flow within me.

Dolnichar was a good speaker. He spoke out loud and clear, composed good sentences, knew where to lay emphasis, a pretty rare thing among us. "Once again the enemy has shattered his teeth and claws in this land of ours..." The invader had come with rumbling tanks and armored cars, withdrawing divisions of crack troops from distant battlefields, supporting them with artillery and aircraft. And what had he achieved? Our resistance was more firm than ever, our troops had gained valuable experience from this latest action, and the link between the people's army and the populace is stronger than ever before. "We shall smite the invader at his every step, and his lackeys too, until at last the day of victory dawns. The army of national liberation has grown from its units, detachments and battalions into a well-organized regular army, the shock troops of our downtrodden populace; its corps, divisions and brigades incessantly harry the foe, demolishing the roads and railways which serve to transport the enemy's men and materials to the front; the whole country is a hornet's nest of furious resistance. The victorious Red Army is driving the enemy back to Berlin. The serpent is in his death throes. Death to Fascism." In response, his listeners roared, "Liberty to the people!"

An accordionist now began to play, with a guitar accompaniment; both the musicians were partisans. Some distance away, large bonfires were blazing, with men and children collecting wood from all sides. A large tricolor with a red star at its center was hanging from the hayrack, tossed and fluttering in the breeze from the mountain tops. Horses stood under the trees, gazing with bright eyes into the flames.

Did the uncertainty about my future spoil that evening for me perhaps? What is it about a human being's make-up that suddenly turns him, for no apparent reason, from a talkative extrovert into a taciturn introvert? What is it that snuffs out his joyful high spirits? What dark premonitions beset his soul? Suddenly, he finds that nothing is going right. What was said a half-hour ago comes back again to mind, but what had then been full of life is now dull and lifeless.

Anton's early account of Spain came back to me again, much clearer now than when I had first heard it. The Spanish are one of those peoples whose particular faults suit them very well. They can sing of death so eloquently that you fall in love with it. They have invented a way of fighting fear, though they are so much in love with life. Those ceremonies of theirs are nothing other than a yearning to preserve life. They turn everything into a ceremony, though they are, at heart, a most simple people. The Germans, by their nature, take courage for granted, and for them so-called heroism is almost a duty. The Spaniards have their own virility rite, which is simply a fight against fear. They love animals. If you say they torment and murder bulls, I will tell you that I would not mind being a Spanish bull destined for death in the arena. At least I would know what was awaiting me. And when I am slain in the arena, every gesture has its name, every movement its technical term, and the death blow is the *coup de grâce*. Elsewhere they rhapsodize about mankind, but no bands play when you are led to the slaughter. You disappear without fuss. A bull is reared, tended, has his great aim in life. But as for us...

In Spain, no one would steal your rifle. A Spaniard propped his gun against the wall of the trench and went home to his wife and children. He had something to eat, something to drink, sang a song, beat up his wife, came back again—and there was his rifle, waiting in the same spot where he had left it. Blood, death, love, curses, prayers, it is all there tied up in the same sack with a Gordian knot; cruelty, tenderness, pity, ecstasy, love and hate, idleness and industry, all bound up inextricably. What methods of torturing prisoners (on both sides)—and what respect for family, forefathers, children! How they manage to talk of the past, have the present day in view, and put everything off till tomorrow! Those devils are never bored. They lie with such style they believe themselves; that mixture of Moors and Latins has produced something other nations find hard to understand. Here we like things plain, like a new string with no knots in it.

Why then did you fall in love with Spain, Anton? What? Do you think I fell in love? With that writing with knots on old string? After all I've seen and read about, from the conquistadors to the last century? What should I fall in love with? With the sultry Madrid summer, when weeks and weeks pass without a breath of air, when you go to sleep with your hand in this position and wake up to find a palm print in sweat? With that awful retreat across the Pyrenees? With their architecture—in war-time you have as little interest in it as in the landscape. With their songs? With the stench of my own body? It's true that I always wanted to see Spain. But with my present vision. Have you seen Ljubljana, down there below us?

As if you could almost touch those lights with your hand...

A town like any other town in the world but you've spent part of your life there. I think that Spain is something similar for us, although its sounds and atmosphere are different. Even the horses there have a different snort.

I know, my girl's not like the others—she smells different, sounds different. Same thing, isn't it?

I was sitting there in a wee courtyard, matchbox size, stone, an old olive tree, a vine and some roses, and a small well. Jacinto was playing some stringed instrument with only three strings, we were drinking sweet wine, a canary was fluttering in a cage hung up in the olive tree, there was a lamp—really, it all didn't amount to much, we were eating bread and cheese. Zharko said he would take the whole place away in his kit-bag as a souvenir. It was very much the same there as here—the war had passed us by, had receded into the background.

But Spain is such a large country, I said, I've seen more extensive olive groves. Why do they build themselves such pokey little courtyards? Our gentry have fine, large gardens around their villas, but you never see them sitting under the trees. That's the secret. That and the weather, the rocky country and the rest of it. You can melt away in those Spanish nights, and afterwards they follow you. You don't know how little a human being requires.

I do.

Translated by Harry Lemming.

An excerpt from
The Great Bear

Miloš Mikeln

Štefan Vidovič was among the first to travel the Savinja Valley to Hudinja and on through the plain of the Celje basin toward the villages Vojnik and Frankolovo.

It was the expansion of the hop fields that tempted him: great earnings from hops. In 1923, hop growers got ninety dinars a kilo for dried hops, in 1924 only seventy-five dinars, and then in 1925 again ninety, and in 1926, just over eighty dinars. So, they said, the price would be sometimes higher and sometimes a little lower, one had to be prepared for that, but with no other crop was it possible to earn anything like so much money. Three kilos of hops amounted to the monthly wage of a farm girl. Or for a kilo of hops, a cubic meter and a half of sawed softwood. And eleven dinars for one Swiss franc: the Savinja landowners of those times were no strangers to the exchange rate for the Swiss franc, or the English pound.

But Štefan could not survive the fall in the price of hops in 1927, by half, to forty dinars a kilo. Especially since he had held off selling too long at that price, and the price had fallen still further, so in the end he got barely twenty-four dinars a kilo. He had set up his hop growing in 1924, on short-term credit, calculating that he would be able to pay it all off from the first complete year in which the hops came to full fruition. When he had taken the credit, he calculated that he would have to sell at eighty dinars in 1927 in order to pay off the loan.

However, when he got less than a third of this, his accounts went completely into the red. Actually, a gaping red hole. First it swallowed his new hop fields. Then the new drier failed, the finest between Celje and Vojnik; it had been erected by the Celje builder, Gologranc, but now nobody needed new hops driers, and it went for hardly more than the used bricks themselves were worth. Finally, he had to sell his real, his original business, the brickworks, to pay off the debt. He was left with only the master's house in Hudinja.

Even the Savinja hop growers of course groaned, but this first weak year and the steep fall in price did not ruin them, since they did not plow, set up hop poles, do the binding or gathering on land bought on credit, or dry in proud new driers built on credit. Some of them were entirely without debts on the estates, because they had paid off the old ones in the first three postwar years, when the produce had a high price and the depreciation of money was under control. Others, burdened with interest, had to take new loans, smaller or even larger, when their anticipated income fell. Large scale indebtedness, and the ruin of hop growing, came only later, in the great crisis of the first half of the thirties. Štefan was one of the few who was flattened in the sudden halving of the price of hops in 1927, and the old hop growers quietly acceded to the ruin of these speculators, as they called them.

Concurrently with his business collapse, there also ended the brief period of his "national endeavors and activities," as a political career was called when mentioned sympathetically.

The first period after the war, for some two years—in some places a little longer, in some a little less—people lived in some sort of strange dizziness. In many families, the old familiar order of life had been destroyed because of those that had fallen in the war—husbands, sons, brothers—or because of the sick and the invalid that the battlefields had sent back home. Elsewhere, everything was turned upside down because of the collapse of the old state and the great changes this transformation had brought: the heads of families lost their jobs, and with them their daily bread; everyone had to seek new employment—not just state officials and those in public service—and suddenly found themselves back at the beginning of life or in a completely different, new job. Even those of independent means, farmers or small businessmen or traders, saw the values on which they had always relied collapse before their very eyes: farm hands were suddenly heedless, maids wanton, and the world out of order. On the other hand, a lot of people sensed the opportunity for a speedy rise, by trade, business, or through conscientious service to the new authorities, and they ruthlessly exploited it. And many were giddy simply from national fervor; it was the end of foreign domination, there was a new free state with brother Croats and Serbs, and great meetings, and flags, everything beginning anew—how could a man not cry out "Cheers" night and day?

People who were poor and without property were still in a special mood, which aroused fear in them and, at the same time, united them: hatred of masters. The war had brought them nothing but suffering—the hunger of the women at home, death or injury to the men at the front—and who but the masters had propelled the world into this crisis? The governing classes, they were newly called. And the governing classes were considered to embrace all people of standing, any kind of master, lay or clerical, mayors and priests, landowners and merchants, officers and attorneys, policemen and postal officials and engineers in factories. The revolutionary spirit which the men and boys had brought back from the front, from Russian captivity and from other scenes of revolution and subversion, was there.

New customs spread: no longer did a man bow and doff his cap when he met a master—in the new world, even a pauper was equal to a man of means, and held his head up high and looked through him as if he simply weren't there. Disdain for all and any kind of men of quality, heedlessness, obstinacy and stubborn wilfulness, these were suddenly the new virtues of simple people.

Mayors and parish priests said, "This will pass, let them calm down and forget the war and revolutionary manners, then we will again rein in our hot-headed Slovenian men."

But in Celje, for the moment, the reins drew constantly to the left. The Social Democrats were strong. The Celje Social Democrats hosted pan-Slovenian meetings and even congresses. The party could have had a great influence on local politics in the first post-war years—if there could be any local politics in the post-war confusion and turmoil.

Inasmuch as there was, Štefan Vidovič, landowner and businessman, also found himself embroiled. He became a Social Democratic municipal councillor, in a fairly unusual way.

On the penultimate day of December 1919, Štefan had barely properly taken over his new company, the brickworks, when he discovered all twenty of his workers, in the middle of the afternoon, gathered around an upturned empty barrel, on which stood a three-liter wicker flask of wine and a glass. The foreman was pouring wine into the glass and saying, "Well, who'll be first," and then in embarrassment, when he caught sight of the master, "Mr. Vidovič, why don't you be first, though it's a workers' holiday..."

"Why not," said Štefan, "even though it's a workers' holiday. What holiday is it?"

They all laughed.

"Well, what holiday it is, the day will tell," and Štefan drained the proffered glass.

"There's no holiday, he's made it up."

"Who?"

They immediately fell silent and exchanged glances, as if they now wanted to help a comrade in distress and not denounce him to the master. "Me," came the slow reply from the one who had earlier been pouring, and had offered the first glass. "I'm Matija Klančar."

"I know, Klančar. So, what kind of holiday?"

"The first anniversary since the national government of Slovenia proclaimed the law on the eight-hour working day."

Some of them laughed again, as if they did not really think to see the master fall victim to an innocent childish prank. "And why not, since it's a holiday," said Štefan. "Another glass, please, it's good wine." They were relieved; one after another they drained the glasses, and the bulging flask was all at once empty. "Now I'll provide the second," said Štefan, "and a couple of loaves of bread and half a kilo of bacon. It will be here soon, we'll finish it off in half an hour, and then we'll get back to honest work. Till the end of the eight-hour day..."

"Of course, Mr. Vidovič."

"Long live Mr. Vidovič!"

"From New Year's on, here in my brickworks it will apply." Štefan fell silent, the enthusiasm subsided in an instant, they waited for him to punish them for their arbitrary holiday; disappointed and distrustful faces stared at him. "It will apply that on Saturdays and days before holidays, we'll work only to noon, but you'll be paid the full eight hours for these six-hour days. That will be my contribution, a further step forward from what the national government of Slovenia began a year ago."

They so mobbed him that he was almost suffocated in the crush, then they raised him on their shoulders and carried him all around the large courtyard of the brickworks; it was almost like an intercessionary procession for the blessing and success of their work, from the moist piles of clay to the kilns. What it was like in detail nobody could later remember exactly, but it was long talked about in Hudinja and Celje.

Štefan's brickworks was henceforth the only company for miles around where they worked only six hours on a Saturday, for eight hours' pay. Because of that, the other businessmen looked askance at the Hudinja Vidovič, as if he were overpaying his workers at their expense. Those who felt that way were mostly owners of small factories, whose workers still for the most part worked a nine-hour day, in some places twelve hours, and sometimes, with well-filled order books, even on Sunday afternoons, so that now some young chaplains waxed indignant in the Sunday sermon against ruthless masters for whom profit was the first and only sacred thing, that they disregarded even the Lord's day.

In the spring of 1920, Matija Klančar asked Štefan whether he would join the Social Democrats and whether they could count on him for the elections to the constitutional assembly for which they were preparing. Štefan said that they could. In the autumn, when there were the real elections, although they had not made him a candidate, he attended and spoke at a number of election meetings. Once, Bara also went with him. She became excited and would have herself stepped onto the speaker's platform, would have spoken heatedly, like that time in the inn at Čakovec where they had first met, thought Štefan in surprise. Her eyes fairly blazed when she stood up and raised her hand, but the men chairing the meeting did not let her speak: things had not come so far that a woman could speak at an election meeting—they don't even have the right to vote, and they want to teach us?

Thereafter, Bara did not attend political gatherings. In December 1922, she gave birth to a second son. They called him Miha, and he was not taken to be baptized either; it would have been necessary to show a marriage certificate, which, in view of their pagan wedding, they of course did not have. It was the same with the third, born in 1925, again at the Three Kings. He was named, what else, Boltežar. Since during the entire pregnancy they had only discussed girls' names, firmly convinced that they would get a daughter on the third time round, when they had to tell Gašper and Miha what their brother was called, and when it was also necessary to announce the name to the house, to the servants and maids, they decided in a moment and so announced Boltežar.

Štefan was at that time deeply involved in politics.

In the spring of 1921 he had been for the first time, and in the summer of 1924 for the second, elected as one of the Social Democratic councillors of the municipality of Celje District. At the elections in 1927, he was replaced by an innkeeper from the Maribor road who, just before the elections, had set up a bold white chapel in front of his inn and then, in speeches at the election meetings, had announced that he had done this for the salvation of his socialist opponent, Štefan Vidovič: he was sorry for him and would do even more to raise a man from hell at least to purgatory, since Štefan Vidovič, the well-known atheist and Bolshevik, would undoubtedly end up there, where, as was well known, all socialists would be consigned, as well as those who recklessly voted for them.

Štefan lost the election for two reasons: just before the elections he resigned from the Catholic Church, more by coincidence than design, and—and this was perhaps even worse—the word had spread that he was about to go bankrupt.

People, though, even without chapels, no longer voted for socialist candidates, workers and foremen on the socialist list, among whom Štefan, as the only businessman, was more or less a rare bird.

When the post-war turmoil died down, arrogance abated. The mayors and priests had been right—let them have their fling, then we'll tame them again—and the revolutionary spirit drowned in the everyday difficulties of life, the voters again voted for the big landowners, lawyers, large merchants and other successful men, even though they had to earn their bitter bread from them. Or perhaps precisely because of it: those who knew how to arrange things best for themselves will also know how to do so for the municipality and for all of us; that's how it is in the world. And if you want work and bread, don't presumptuously resist those who know better.

The "godless socialists"—at least that part of the work force which was more strongly bound to tradition, to the land, to the church and religion—when the post-war revolt and wilfulness had passed, slowly returned to the clerical side and once more began to respect God, authority and property. On the other hand, the socialists themselves also changed. The most pugnacious Social Democrats began to join the Communists. Those not inclined to revolution and communism joined the Christian trade unions and thus came closer to authority than to opposition. Those who remained in the center, the center-minded Social Democrats who believed in the gradual development of workers' solidarity and in political activity in the parliamentary parties, slowly but steadily lost power and influence. The people in Slovenia also unwittingly followed the currents of the times which began to prevail throughout Europe, and these led only to extremism, right or left. There was no longer any real space for those tending toward the center.

Štefan's famous departure from the Church came about by accident, because of the baptismal certificate of his eldest son, Gašper, who was enrolled in primary school in that year. The parents, of course, had to submit the baptismal certificate on enrollment. They did not have it, and so Gašper Vidovič came to school as the only one of his class without this document. Štefan's excuse of the post-war confusion, in which the child had been left without documents certifying his birth and baptism, did not help at all. Finally, the school administrator said, "Let the child be baptized again; better two baptisms than to be without papers." Štefan didn't say that, in fact, he would have liked to have had him baptized already, but of course this would not work either because the parents lacked a marriage certificate. He went from the school to the mayor's office, and from the mayor's office to the parish priest, and was finally directed to the Abbot of Celje, Peter Jurak.

Jurak was a strict man. During the war he had served as a chaplain at the front, and a little of the officer's manner remained with him forever. However, he was also a fair man. People respected him.

When, after a first unsuccessful call for applications in 1921, the Maribor episcopacy for a second time called for applications for the position of Abbot of Celje in 1923, Dr. Anton Korošec and Peter Jurak applied. The Maribor bishop, Karlin, probably did not want a politician in this influential Church position in the county of Celje, and he resolved the quandary by rejecting both applications. There was a third call for applications in August 1924. Nobody applied, but at the Bishop's persuasion, on the last day, Jurak lodged a request for appointment, and Dr. Korošec, as the Belgrade Minister of Religious Affairs, confirmed his appointment.

But for all his fairness and understanding of human pressures, in matters of faith Jurak was uncompromising. He could not issue a certificate of baptism, he declared outright, and he could not recognize their marriage. He would be prepared to marry them if they first performed all that was necessary for a man and woman who had lived so long in sin: a serious confession and a long penance.

Then Štefan stood up violently and raised both hands: "So, I had to serve the most Catholic of all emperors for five years, three of them at the front—and before they sent me there, the archbishop of Ljubljana himself blessed the boys who humbly gave themselves to be driven to death—and when in the post-war confusion my present wife saved my life, riddled by bullets, on the point of death, and I married her, we couldn't get God's blessing because the priest there had locked himself in and barricaded the door of his rectory with great beams, in fear lest someone empty his granary and hen-house, and wouldn't even show himself at the window when they called him for a baptism or funeral, let alone a wedding—and now you'd impose penance on the two of us for that?"

Then he forced himself to calm down and said slowly, the words falling one upon another, with long intervals, as if piling heavy stones onto a heap, that he had had enough of it all, and that he was quitting the Church and the faith.

Abbot Jurak, white as a sheet, was silent at the table before him for a long time. "If that's what you want, Mr. Vidovič, consider how it will publicly shame your brother, who is an honorable and temperate man. But alright. Return your certificate of baptism to the parish priest's office, here, and submit a note with the request that you be struck from the list of believers of the Lavantine episcopacy and the Roman Catholic Church."

The quiet but sharp words of the abbot affected Štefan more than an angry reply to his violent outburst would have. But what's said is said. He curtly nodded and, briefly thanking him, left.

It appeared that even the abbot himself didn't know everything, namely that a certificate of baptism and a note are not a weighty enough official reason for such an arbitrary act. Štefan had to lodge at the district board a stamped request to the Ministry of the Interior in Belgrade, in order to register his departure from the Church. The district board rejected his request several times in succession and sent it to the competent mayor of the municipality of Celje District, comrade Valentin Hrastnik, a socialist and foreman at the Westen enamelware factory. He initially returned it to the district officer, without telling Štefan anything about it, and then submitted that "Mr. Štefan Vidovič recognize the complete impropriety of his intended act and desist from the same."

Hrastnik tried to persuade Štefan above all that, as an unbeliever, he would destroy his future for all time: if he ever needed work, for instance, he would certainly not obtain it. Štefan stuck to his guns and demanded a "civil baptismal document" for his sons. After thinking it over, Mayor

Hrastnik knew of no better way, and for all three sons at the same time so that he wouldn't have the same problems with the other two later. But even this took time. The municipality gave him some sort of temporary paper with which Gašper could be enrolled in the first class. Only after a year did Štefan obtain a document which confirmed that he had been officially removed from the Roman Catholic Church.

Of course, this was all discussed at length throughout Celje. And of course, after that, he had no chance in the elections: only some of the most convinced opponents of Church involvement in social, educational and other civil affairs voted for him, and even these were more from the ranks of the old liberals than from the Social Democrats. Although the latter were not on good terms with the Church, they preferred to avoid conflict with it, since they had already barely avoided the bad reputation of atheism among the people, who regarded faith, the Church and everything connected with it as an inevitable framework in which man's life from birth to death unfolded. They immediately closed their ears distrustfully to anyone who demonstrated a real intention to withdraw from or even destroy this framework, which was consecrated with the gilding of centuries, and was each time renewed with brilliant ceremonies in the confidence-inspiring eternal rhythm of the change of seasons.

His business ruin was more serious than his political one.

For some months after this, after fairly quick bankruptcy proceedings in which he had lost everything except the large villa in which they lived, they could still survive on what Bara had in the cellar and storehouse, and some money which could still be found here and there, mostly from previously unfinished business. But even this modest source was soon exhausted, and from the kitchen there wafted throughout the whole house only the smell of potatoes and cabbage. He had to find work.

"Of course, Mr. Vidovič, I would take you on with pleasure, Mr. Vidovič, but you know, a businessman cannot afford to have his clients look askance at him, which would be inevitable, God preserve us, if he were to employ a man without..., well, you know, without moral principles, without respect for the faith, as you know very well yourself..."

Some of them even said straight out: "What did you have to do it for? Did anyone force you to go to evensong or sing in the choir? To go to church to get married and have your children baptized, that you could surely have endured, couldn't you? But you preferred to start all this circus and leave the Church and everything. And you know, you've only yourself to blame.

And just when your brother has become mayor and all sorts of fine, profitable business might have come your way..."

Štefan had become so accustomed in the last months to being humiliated and sometimes even to being treated with open scorn, that he heard such sermons to the end and then, without answer, turned and left.

But at night, alone or with Bara by his side, when he did not know whether she were sleeping or hiding her misery from him and not showing that the nights were even more bitter for her, despair overcame him. Good, the house was still here. But since he had already sought a buyer for it, and they would get little enough for it, it would be necessary to move somewhere, and when the money from the sale was gone, they would no longer even have a roof over their head. And what then? Would he go and beg his brother in Breg to take him under his roof, give him shelter in a shed or the cellar, like a beggar? Would he take his wife and three children to Metlika or Lokvica, all in a single room or perhaps even just in the haybarn above some stables? And what was there, anyway? Would anyone still know him and would they have corn and potatoes at least to assuage their hunger?

He felt guilty about his wife and three children. Where were the times when he had quickly loaded all four into the coach some afternoon and driven them into town for errands, or even just for the fun of it? Or when, for example, he had taken all three boys to the barber for the first time? Until then Bara had cut the two older boys' hair herself when it got too long. When the youngest, Bolt, had been ready for her scissors, Štefan had said that that would no longer do, that from then on they would go to a real barber. Not to some bungler in Hudinja or Bukovžlak, but to a real master in the town. Bara wanted to go with them, but he did not take her: this was not for a woman, just as a man did not enter a hairdressing salon. So they went by themselves. The first suitable barber was just as they entered the town, but there was nowhere to leave the coach there. He turned right immediately after the credit bank, but as if in spite, there was no barber on the entire street. He did not consider searching on toward the hospital, but turned back toward the center of the town and into the narrow street behind the theater toward the Turkish Cat, and from there to the left and into the square behind the Old Pot, where there were enough tetherings for horses, which were often left there by people coming into town for errands. He tied up the team and gave them hay, and then all three went past the Turkish Cat. On the corner where there was an enticing smell of fresh bread and biscuits, the boys would not stop their pestering until he stopped at the bakery and bought them each a bun, and then they turned toward the town hall and the German church, so that finally they were within a dozen steps of the barber. "Amand Pepernik, shaving and haircutting," read the eldest Gašper aloud, and the younger two, who were not yet up to letters, believed him literally. The boys became very serious, fear was visible in the eyes of all three, but they courageously walked behind their father and then, one after another, bravely sat in the large shaving chair fitted with dangerous levers. Štefan sat with the other two behind each hero of the experience in turn, and pretended that it was all nothing, but every instant sought in the mirror the gaze of the sufferer on the chair, smiled at him and conspiratorially winked, and the boys gratefully answered him with long, devoted looks, to which they added forced, brave smiles. "Did they cry and shriek terribly, because they always cry the first time?" asked Bara when they returned home, and the boys proudly feigned anger: after all, why would anyone shriek, it wasn't anything, come on, Mama. Štefan was seized with a mood of celebration and poured the boys some sweet raspberry cordial and gave them each a piece of chocolate, and Bara and he opened a bottle of wine, as if they were celebrating a holiday.

Yes, where were those times? It had been a long time since there had been money in the house for a bottle of wine. Or for the barber, which actually cost more for all three heads than a bottle of Riesling. That the three Vidovič boys walked around with long hair, like the Indians in the new Metropol cinema on King Peter Road, was one of the least painful effects of the dearth which had settled upon the large house in Hudinja. Štefan almost never saw Bara any more except in tears. She cried in the morning when he left and in the evening when he returned from his unsuccessful search for work.

When he again unsuccessfully registered at the employment office and aimlessly wandered toward the meadow behind the grammar school and the Protestant church, he was stopped by a gentleman in an impeccable black coat, small in build but upright in stance: "*Guten Tag, Herr Vidovič. Ich bin Doktor Gerhard May.*"

"Good day, minister. There's no need to introduce yourself, please, since I know you. Who in Celje doesn't know you?"

They spoke in German: the Protestant minister of Celje, Dr. May, would on no account speak a word of Slovenian. Štefan's German had never been good, and in recent years he had almost forgotten the little he knew, but Pastor May was used to that: even his flock, the Celje protestant Germans, with rare exceptions, did not speak proper German.

"I hear you're looking for work, Mr. Vidovič, but without success."

"So, the word has reached you, too, has it?"

"Oh, we know everything."

Štefan looked askance. The minister laughed and waved his hand, as if to say they'd not discuss that, and continued seriously. "You can't find work because you didn't want to get married and baptize your children according to the Catholic rites. Well, of course, in Prekmurje, from where you brought your wife, there are plenty of Protestants, which these ignorant people in Celje don't know, *nicht wahr*, eh."

"You know that, too, hmm? But my wife is not actually from Prekmurje, and she's also not, how shall I say, of your Protestant faith..."

"You see, even we didn't know that. I thought that she was a Protestant. Never mind. I think I can help you anyway."

"How can you help me?"

"With a good job."

"Yes?"

"Yes."

"Well, my leaving the Church came about more by accident than design, I think, not from any special conviction... So, I don't intend... To be blunt... I'm sorry, my German is really very bad..." Štefan in truth was less in search of the right words than trying to cover his embarrassment.

"Be blunt. You don't intend to enter the Protestant faith, you wanted to say."

"Well, yes."

"You don't have to. We're not going to employ you as cantor in the church, so it's all the same what faith you are. You don't have to be rebaptized, though even that is not so difficult for others, as we've both been able to see now that some of the prominent Celje families have eagerly entered the Serbian Orthodox faith. That doesn't count with me. The Germans are a civilized nation. You're an able young man, and it's a pity for such a man to be without work."

"Whether I'm able or not is—"

"Oh, we know about your hops disaster. You're not the only one, you know. You may be the first, but not the last. There will be many who'll go bankrupt yet. There's a crisis coming; times will be bad. So a good job will be that much more worth having. But to come to the point. Rakusch ironworks need a competent traveling salesman. The pay will be on commission. It won't be difficult for you to sell good Rakusch ware. You're a smart fellow. Your name, and that of your brother the mayor, doesn't worry us. On the contrary: both the owners, the Messrs. Rakusch, excellent Germans and proud to be German, are of course first and foremost merchants, and here in this country even a German trader needs Slovenian customers, so in this case the interests of the firm and your circle of acquaintances match perfectly. I'm not talking here as an ignorant pastor but as a good friend of the house and firm of Rakusch. You're not involved in politics any more?"

"No."

"I understand you. You see, the Slovenians didn't get all they wanted in this state."

"Oh, it wasn't that..."

"Wasn't it? Well, you haven't yet considered it altogether. Since the Balkan wars in 1912 and 1913, Serbia has been only concerned with digesting its southern provinces. And looking still further south, to Salonika. They're not concerned with the Slovenians, nor with the Croats in Istria, Dalmatia and the islands, occupied by Italy. In 1918, they would have sold the whole of Slovenia and half of Croatia for Salonika if they could have got it. Yes, they only gaze down there, like an overfed dog at the smell of a sausage which it would like to gobble up but can't manage any more. They won't get it either, but all the same, they can't take their eyes off it. Let me tell you something, Mr. Vidovič, the only ones who can live together with the Serbs are those on the same economic and cultural level, or a little lower. Do you know why? Because they make the law for the whole country according to their own needs. Anyone who has more than they have, they take it away. Only for those with the same or less, only for such are their laws and customs to the right measure: they won't take from such people, because their measure applies to themselves, too, and they don't take from themselves. Do you understand? No? Well, that's an understanding that awaits you. I've given you a little too long a lecture here in the middle of the street. Among the others of us, the Styrian Germans don't understand you Slovenians as I do. Although I lead the Kulturbund here, I still acknowledge the Slovenian nation for what it is. It certainly deserves a better fate. I think that Serbia is ruthlessly exploiting it. But never mind politics. The house of Rakusch needs a good traveling salesman with a prominent name, and you a good job and money..."

"A job?"

"A well-paid job."

Štefan didn't even try to hide his excitement. However, he would have to consider whether employment with a German firm wouldn't do him more harm than good. But what of it? Weren't the majority, or at least half of the Celje shops in the hands of Germans? Not to mention the factories, Westen, one thousand two-hundred workers, Slovenian to a man working for the Germans and happy enough to have the work.

"Well, you don't have to decide here on the street. Think it over for a week, and then... So, Mr. Vidovič, we've conversed long enough, have we not, and now we must each go our own way."

Štefan automatically reached into his breast pocket for his watch. It wasn't there any longer; he had sold it the previous week and got barely a tenth of its real value for it.

When a man has already sold his watch, he's in no position to be choosy about a job. He buttoned up his jacket, straightened up, as if coming to attention, and asked, "When can I start?"

Translated by Martin Creegan.

An excerpt from
Filio is Not at Home

Berta Bojetu-Boeta

A long time passed. Nothing happened. Until last night. There was a knock on the door. I knew it was him.

I felt like a long distance runner. I had run a strenuous race, and deserved to win. If they allowed me to open the school, two or three classes perhaps, I would achieve my purpose and would grow old peacefully. I had little time left. Not enough to leave or attempt new changes.

When I opened the door I was nervous as a runner at the start of a race. He carried a wooden box that concealed his face. He placed it on the floor under the window and turned to me. He put his arm around my shoulders and led me to the bed. We sat down. I folded my hands in my lap and waited. I was certain I had permission to open the school and needed to compose myself so as not to blurt out something foolish. I had come a long way but hardly felt the sweet taste of victory. Years of hard labor, fear of not knowing where the next blow would come from, had taken their toll on me.

"Here are the textbooks. You are not allowed to use anything else. Such is the condition," he pointed at the box. "Dirana is well supplied with notebooks. I have all the required documents. The seal and the forms for grading are in the box. Everything is in order. You will manage. Find help. Take over the higher grades. Let someone else teach the lower ones. There aren't many qualified for schooling. You will find that out."

"I didn't expect it to be that easy. I'm amazed."

"The school is of little importance compared to the one on the continent. She is too ignorant about the living conditions here. She heard of you when she was very young. 'Let her do what she wants,' she said to me. 'She cannot leave the island, and the women there could use some education. Prescribe the curriculum. She should follow it strictly. If she doesn't, ban the school.' The factory down there," he pointed in the direction of the Lower town, "is in trouble. I have a hard time finding people to do the work. They are either stupid, sick, or running away. I don't like it, I would like to retire. Yes, a little more knowledge. Perhaps Uri will take over. Just don't get too excited. I worry seeing joy on your face; it always brings trouble. As long as I live, or until I receive different orders, nothing will change here."

That was all. He left. And yet he was my friend.

*　　*　　*

Today I walked through the town, I needed to find a suitable house for the school. It's been a while since I had a good look at the town. I had already forgotten that each renovated house meant one more woman who was no longer at the mercy of Kata and her slaves. I thought of that year when the town was stirred up by change and persecution.

I found the house behind the church. Because the house had no railings, I hardly ever wandered there. The house looked like a school with four class-rooms, and that's what it probably had been years before. It had stood abandoned for many years. The unlocked door screeched and tore loose a big cobweb when I pushed it open. I looked around and made up my mind on the spot.

In the afternoon I waited for Lana. She supervised vegetable deliveries from the kitchen to the stairway. That wasn't really her duty, but she was replacing a sick woman. We both put our everyday duties aside and devoted ourselves to preparations for the school.

The house was in good condition. It remained sturdy and strong behind the closed shutters but needed cleaning and painting. I asked my women to help me. In a few days they had it all cleaned and ready for a paint job.

*　　*　　*

Today I set off toward the school at the crack of dawn. When I turned the church corner I saw Kata. She was standing by the door, waiting for me. She was bending the indispensable stick in her hands. Just like a bailiff. She did not intimidate me. I approached her, carrying two buckets of lime. Lana stood at the end of the hallway, holding a large bucket of water. She waited to see what would happen. The hideous creature by the door did not let me pass. I saw determination in her catlike eyes. I dropped one bucket and held the other as a shield. I didn't know what exactly to expect, but I felt she would attack me at any moment. And she did. A stick came driving through the air. At that point Lana appeared at the door. She dropped the bucket and shoved Kata past me. Her huge body fell flat on the ground; her long legs and underpants showed from under her skirt. The elastic bands holding her stockings up were stretched and filthy and looked incredibly distasteful. She became aware of it and started to pull the short skirt to her knees. She looked ridiculous and helpless as she tried to pick herself up. It was then that Lana leaned toward her from the threshold and splashed a bucketful of water into her face. She had a difficult time getting up. She was heavier and less agile than she used to be. It gave me time to collect and prepare myself. I looked at Lana. She stood upright, her head lifted high. Waiting. The empty bucket hung in her hand, water dripping down the doorstep, forming a puddle. That's how we meet our destiny, I thought, looking at the woman. She managed to get to her knees, stood up, spat at us and left. It was an odd picture; she was disappearing down the street, dripping wet, thrusting her body forward in an awkward way. Poor thing, I thought briefly. Yet I knew in my heart that she wasn't. How she would exhibit her power after this incident I couldn't predict, but I knew she had a great deal of it left, and that she would use it to the last.

*   *   *

Lana and I have been waiting for some days to see what, if anything, might happen. We leaf through the textbooks and are bored. I don't want to start the work until autumn. Perhaps it is best this way. I don't quite want to admit it, but there is something else holding me back. Something troubles me. Something is in the air; it is too quiet. I cannot go on. I feel uneasy about certain women who have through the years only pretended to accept the new order; they knew well that they would otherwise go hungry.

With the school it's different. I can't force them to send their children to school. It was stated in the document I was given that a certain number of children were required for the elementary and secondary school. They can inflict real harm now and will stop at nothing. How to deal with this problem is beyond me. Can the women who are on my side come up with enough children to comply with the condition? I don't know.

They're smarter than I thought. Whose idea was it to get back at me this way? Mare's, Kata's, Lukria's? Lukria has been seen walking gloomily around the town lately. Perhaps there is more to come?

*   *   *

An hour ago Mare entered without knocking. She approached the table of textbooks and rummaged through them. Slowly, as if at home, she picked up one after another, completely ignoring me. I hardly dared breathe. She was aloof and impertinent. She glanced at me every now and then. Her contemptuous smile promised nothing good. After she put down the last book she opened a drawer as if she had known she would find the seal there. She didn't know how to use it. She turned it in her hand like a child examining a new toy. Then she pocketed it and left.

*   *   *

Lana is apparently not giving up. She sits with me for hours, asking questions about the subject matter of the textbooks. She can write and do some math; she has basic knowledge and is a quick learner. Her grandmother was a teacher in the old times. Lana will do. She can help me with the first graders. Perhaps it is all to no avail. All my plans and preparations may be doomed if I don't get the seal back. Disheartened and disappointed, I move from chair to chair to bed, trying to come up with a solution.

*   *   *

This morning was heavy and foggy. I was standing at the back. I still enjoy being among women, still enjoy glimpsing my Master discreetly.

He came, a dark figure. He turned his head slightly to the right, enough to sense me among the crowd. Something traveled between us that would never be lost. I felt happy. He'd opened up to me for a moment, sent me a thought which had to pass me by. Why I would never know.

Behind him walked a young man whom I did not recognize at first. Uri! I was shaken by his beauty, by the oddly dignified beauty that unveiled itself distinctively between his narrow, stubborn shoulders. Only because I knew him could I tell from a distance that he had freckles. He was, so to speak, an even color otherwise. He was brown, all in brown, he looked colorless; so brown that it seemed he was trying to hide, to hide and never be found. He would be hard to spot in the fields on the hill. His hair and clothes were the same color. Only his skin was lighter, like sun-baked soil in the fields. From now on, I'll avoid lingering in front of the church on Sundays.

* * *

I leapt out of a dream and looked around the room. The noise, coming first from the room at the end of the corridor and later from the hall, frightened and paralyzed me for a moment. I got up and peeked into the hall. In front of my daughter's room, two men were shoving each other, cursing through their teeth. I stepped closer, ignorant of what was happening. Enough light penetrated the window for me to recognize one of them. He was the lame one who had, in his impatient manner, limped through the house before. He always arrived before the house settled down for the night. He was always in a hurry, looking hastily for the door, closing it behind him like the master of the house. In the door frame I saw my daughter in a white nightgown, heard her stammer and plead incoherently. Only then did I understand that the two were fighting for a place in her bed. It would never have crossed my mind that she was worthy of a quarrel, let alone a fight. The lame one obviously cared about her, for he didn't give an inch. He beat and kicked the other man, faltered, then finally got rid of him. He closed the entrance door behind him and majestically entered my daughter's room. The leg he dragged behind lingered for a moment on the threshold. My god, how good it would be to have a master in the house.

I couldn't go back to sleep but listened to a long, loud argument for some time. Only later did I drift into dreams. Let her live her own way. She apparently has no desire for me to get involved in her affairs.

* * *

I feel so isolated. It's a holiday, and I have no one to sit with, to say the words which people exchange on such occasions, or to listen to the Master reading words in remembrance. I've been forgotten among certain people, my people have forgotten me, and they'd denounce me if they knew how I lived. I'm therefore isolated. The empty space of nonbelonging has been created for Filio as well. Nothing I can do about it.

I want the days of uncertainty and conflict to pass. I'm tired. Before I lit the oil lamp, I saw a face by the window. An unknown face. I couldn't even tell whether it was a man or a woman. Either could be found beneath my window. One because of Filio, observing her growth, perhaps, the other because of me and the school. The pressure is silent and seemingly harmless. Nothing tangible happens, nothing explicit, but for weeks I've been hiding the signs from Filio, closing my eyes, trying to ignore it. The face at the window came as a final blow. I still haven't recuperated from the morning when I was given a jolt on the doorstep: a large dead fish lay stinking there. It must have been leaning against the door, since it fell on my feet when I opened it. It was still wet and completely rotten. Huge worms were crawling along the stone, making their way to the house. I moaned and turned to the wall. I went back into the house, leaving the fish on the doorstep. I sat down in front of my room in shock, stared in front of me, toward the light. I didn't really see anything but a single thought gnawed at me. What am I doing here? I had forgotten what kept me on the island, so I shook my head, wondering why I hadn't already left. I had also forgotten that I wasn't allowed to leave. I was simply kept there. I'd never expressed these thoughts in words, and had been thus unaware of them.

I'm facing a new problem. I'll deal with it just like the first time; I'm determined to do what I've vowed to do.

Through the light, I saw Lana stepping over the fish. She turned away in disgust, like she couldn't believe her eyes. She sat down next to me, and we must have remained like this for a long time and forgot altogether to go to the school, as was planned. The windows needed washing, and that was the last chore to be done.

I wish I could leave. I loathe this place. Filio came running in from somewhere, all excited. She found us on the threshold, numbly holding one another, with wet cheeks which we started to dry simultaneously. I jumped to my feet and took her into the kitchen. I gave her some bread and cheese, hoping that Lana would dispose of the fish in the meantime.

It's hard. In the evening the tension thickens. I'm more afraid of them than ever before.

* * *

After a few days we walked to the school. Lana clung to me as never before. The town was resting in the early afternoon, gathering strength before evening. I avoided meeting other women. I couldn't trust anybody any longer. But I needed their children. I couldn't possibly school Filio alone. Composed and determined, we walked past closed shutters and doors. At the edge of the square, right next to the church, we suddenly saw a group of women waiting for us. The maid had warned us that they waited there day after day, but we'd forgotten. We walked toward them. Every power is dangerous, and this one was much more so, because it was unknown. We shivered. They hated us both, and I saw they wished to insult and humiliate me. More than that. Some had thick sticks like Kata's ready in their hands.

"Lana, turn around and go home. This is mine to deal with."

"You know I can't. I'll help you. None of them are young. Maybe we can handle them."

What do they have against me and the school? It will be beneficial for the children. Their thoughts cannot reach beyond Kata's orders, I had just enough time to think, before a stick whizzed past my head. I know Kata's reasons, and theirs are simply a consequence. I have to fight. I swung the bucketful of water toward the woman trying to knock me down. I turned here and there, hitting blindly whomever came close. I was lucky I had the bucket. Without it I would have been knocked to the ground. They couldn't come close, either to me or to Lana. Suddenly everything went quiet. They stood around us, and we were turning around, swaying from one foot to the other. We stopped for a moment, and a few of them fled. Three strong women remained, perhaps a year or two younger than us; we clenched our teeth and plunged ahead. We didn't hesitate one bit. I picked up a stick and started beating the first one, then the second, until there was only one left. She was defending herself rather than attacking us. I was hitting her with all my might. I started shouting words about help and suicide. I don't remember what I was saying. It was over only after I threw the bitch onto the ground. She fought well and long. A few times I thought that I myself would fall, surrender, but then I hit her again, beat up the stupid flesh, trying to convey the message to her that I had no intention of stopping.

Lana and I collapsed on some rocks. We were disheveled, our clothes torn. Those women gave up at the right time; I had no strength left. Blood slithered down Lana's forehead, her hair was sticking out in all directions, her lifted skirt was torn, shortened ridiculously at one side, revealing her bare thigh.

My sweet Lana. I smiled at her tired face. She smiled back, and then we burst out laughing. It was a relief from the anxiety and tension. We laughed uncontrollably, looking around to see if anybody was watching. Who else would dare to attack us?

*   *   *

Only today did we wash the windows. The day was pleasant, and nothing out of the ordinary happened. Nothing belongs to me. Not any longer. The life I once had I cast off a long time ago. It's true that a coincidence brought me here, but I still had a choice at the beginning when I was still strong. Now there's no more of "take it or leave it."

For a few days there was no wind. The heavy air lay upon us, pressing us to the ground. There was a stench in the school. We tried to find the source of it, but since it stank in front and around the school as well, we gave up and hurried home.

*   *   *

Behind the windows, still cold from the night, day is dawning. Spring is taking its time this year. Wind forced us from the streets into the houses; only now and then I found relief from its sound. The windows and doors shook, especially during the night; there was no way of knowing whether it was the gale or somebody banging on them. Night after night somebody was banging on the walls and the wood with an iron rod; I heard and recognized the sound. It was both a threat and a warning. After days of this deafening noise, my tired ears can hear but not distinguish anything. Lana hasn't come to see me. Are they torturing her as well? I must go to her today.

*   *   *

The wind has stopped, and so has the banging, which drove me to a corner where I crouched, terrified of everything. They have given up for now; without Lana I wouldn't have managed. Pained and weary, I'm unable to do anything but rest and seek comfort in her.

Days passed, and the fear with them. I glanced from under my eyebrows, expecting another attack. There were no signs of adversity, and I decided to walk to school again. Lana came along. She never left my side.

We opened the shutters and tried to air the stench away. It was unmistakably there. Inside the house. The shutters had been closed for some time, so the smell was shut inside. We could hardly breathe. It was overwhelming. We started searching. We walked through the classrooms, examined the teacher's room, opened closets, drawers, moved desks and rummaged through old papers. There had to be a dead animal somewhere. Except we couldn't find it. With our hands clamped to our noses we walked all over. Then we both suddenly thought of something. The cellar! We hadn't looked there yet; the stench was most likely coming from there. We descended the stairs into the darkness. The stench intensified. We couldn't see anything, so I ran out and opened the cellar window shutters. I heard Lana calling me. Her voice was sad and fearful; it echoed so forbiddingly that I rushed to her. I didn't want to leave her alone for a single moment. I stood behind her, my hands on my mouth. I couldn't believe what I saw. A hairy pile that had collapsed within itself rose before me. Then it dawned on me. It was a large, a very large pile of dead cats. I came apart, perhaps due to the foul air or the cats. Where had Kata ordered them to be collected?

*   *   *

Autumn is near. The evening is hot and stuffy. It presses down, like the darkness inside us. I still don't have the seal. How am I to continue, whom do I turn to? Again, I attempted to talk to them. They turned me down, like a little beggar.

*   *   *

Somebody followed me through the dusk as I was returning home from Lana's. As I reached my door the stalker grabbed me by the shoulders and pushed me against the wall. With my face against the stone I couldn't recognize the force bearing down on me. I felt like a rabbit nailed to a board, waiting to be skinned, pierced by a manure fork and hung on the wall. The feeling took away my willpower. It bode no good. I wanted to survive. The past suddenly became clear. It had a different face than I expected. I became dizzy with anxiety.

"It will be over soon," I heard a man's voice say. "I have to do it quickly, without pleasure, they told me."

He spun me around and bit into my lips. I didn't scream, accepted my fate and waited. After all, it was I who decided to take them on. I knew that the seed was bad. Roses don't grow from thistles. He dragged me into the house, to the room. He, too, knew the way. He pulled a chair from the table and threw me over it. My legs and arms hung from it like a rag. I didn't resist. I let him lift my skirt and take off my panties. I lay still, slumped within myself, oblivious of my own existence. I just waited for it to be over.

What happened halted my thought. I don't know what was worse. He flogged my behind with a stick until I could feel the warmth of my own blood. I clutched the chair and pushed my feet against the floor to prevent myself from pleading and screaming. Then he took me violently from behind, stabbing at me again and again like a pig that wants to break free.

I slid off the chair when he closed the door behind him. I didn't move for a long time. I didn't dress, I just lay there and forgot about everything but the humiliation.

*　　*　　*

"I settled it with them. Here's the seal. I never thought they'd go this far." He threw the seal on the table and left. A few days have passed since that evening. I've recuperated a bit. I'd been feverish, but it passed yesterday. That night I crawled to bed. I kept washing and washing myself, but there seemed never to be enough water in the house to wash away the disgust. It is of no avail: we carry everything with us, nothing is ever lost.

I shuddered when he entered. Indifferent, he threw the seal on the table and left. Did I know him, my Commander? Did I love him? Yes and no. Passion, lust, strangeness and the power of a great ego? I can't recall any feelings, but they must have existed. I no longer know what was real and what wasn't.

I got up after he left. I took the seal in my hands and was happy. Without anger I thought about the women and the man who'd tried to prevent me from opening the school. That was a time of fear; they'd rooted it in me forever. Fate? It was the fate I deserved.

*　　*　　*

School starts tomorrow. I announced it in front of the church, asking women to send the children age eight or older. Girls, that is. I had difficulty placing them. Almost all of them need to be taught how to write. A small light in the darkness. How much of it did I see?

* * *

Today we opened the school and had the first classes. Everything is behind us now. The silent months of stalking and secret informing were devastating.

How many evil things can man come up with to harm those he doesn't approve of? My daughter lies dead in her room. I'm waiting for Lukria to take her away. The door has just opened. It must be her.

She stood at the door when I stepped into the hall. A neatly folded sheet hung from her shoulder. She didn't look at me as she clattered past. I looked after her, appalled. It was hard to believe her nonchalance.

I followed her. Stopped at the door. She was wrapping the corpse with harsh, fast movements, making it jolt like a hard ball. She paid no attention to me, as if it had nothing to do with me. It was devastating to see my daughter's nude body. My chest tightened and I pressed my hands against it for support. I thought I'd collapse. The bruised body belonged to me, and now I was giving it away, in the most improbable way. The woman was doing her job; the more impersonal, cold and detached she was, the more it tore me apart inside. Suddenly I let out a scream and leaped toward her. I yanked the sheet out of her hands, pushing, biting, fighting her. To no avail. In the end she wrapped the corpse and left the room. I collapsed in the corner and sobbed. I had no willpower left to go after her. I stayed where I was. Through tears I saw the maid coming in. I lifted my face.

"How much longer will you just watch her carry them away? How can you be so indifferent?"

She let me have my say then sat down on the floor next to me. She stroked me with gracious gentleness and forgiveness, as if I were a child.

"Those who are hurt have the right to hurt," she said and placed my head in her lap. "Cry, Helena, you can do nothing else now."

"Did you see the man who beat her up?" I asked. "It was the one who was a frequent visitor here, the lame one, wasn't it? He finished her off with a rock. Did you get that rock?"

"It's there, under the table," she pointed to the floor.

I followed her pointing finger with my eyes and saw a large stone, covered with blood, lying there like a witness, waiting to be hidden. I crawled to it and put it in my apron. I crawled back and leaned against the wall. Between my legs, in my lap, I felt the horrid weight of the blows which had killed that simple being, my daughter. She was like a chapel. Without memories. She was entered, passed by, nobody left anything in her, only a scratch here and there. She seemed to be her own purpose.

She hated me. She made it clear she didn't want to have anything to do with me. We avoided one another. She hardly knew Filio. Now Lukria had taken her away, and I felt that the house would be empty. I loved her after all. Filio was her flesh and blood. "Is Filio asleep?" I asked.

"She's been asleep for some time. I carried her upstairs," I heard the maid say, thinking of the girl who was bequeathed to me. The maid and I had put Filio on the chest by my daughter's bed, to have them both near when we treated my daughter's wounds. In the morning, Filio fainted when she saw her mother all beaten up; it was the first time ever my daughter had Filio in her room. She whispered to me to let Filio stay with her.

I brought her daughter to her. Filio didn't wake up while we bandaged her mother's wounds. The maid and I were shaking her, trying to wake her, but nothing worked. I left the room for a moment. When I returned, my daughter was dead, and Filio lay on the floor by her bed. She must have woken up and fainted again. Poor child.

*　　*　　*

Uri comes more and more frequently. He returns books promptly and takes out new ones. It must be hard for him in the prison where he works. He looks pale and in need of sleep. It's dismal. Today his visit was brief. Usually he sits by the window and discusses the books, paces the room and when it is time to go, leaves dissatisfied. Today we just sat. No words were necessary. I sat next to him, leaning on the wall, looking through the window at the sea. My eyes traveled with him to the horizon and beyond. What places did our minds wander to today? Perhaps we both longed for towns and their splendor. But differently. He doesn't know the people out there. I once knew them. They're no good. And if there are any good ones, it's too late to look for them. He can, perhaps, still find them.

*   *   *

I felt heavy when I got up. I hurried, though some strange premonition weighed me down, making it hard to move. Somebody has been frequenting the house for weeks. Doors are being slammed inconsiderately, as if someone were angry. I don't know what's happening, but a thought has struck me which I don't dare say out loud. Are they looking for Filio?

She's fifteen. Can it be that she's already included in the labyrinth of nocturnal visits? And what am I to do if she is? Can I prevent them? To think that men might again promenade around the house, old and young, sleazy and loathsome, robust or awkward, lying with my girl. She's tall, slender and fragile. I worry about her. I believe she doesn't care for all these bodies and smells. She's a quiet and bright girl. Deep in her thoughts, she does her chores around the house. She grew up so suddenly. The years have gone by and I hardly noticed where I lived. All but a faint anxiety was erased. I'm no longer included in their lives, have given up everything but the school.

I see Uri often. We have deep discussions about the books we read. He's a man now, though he still lets me stroke his curly head.

Where can I hide Filio? We can no longer run away. It's too late.

*   *   *

This time, too, she stood at the door like an admonition. The years have shriveled her, only the wickedness in her posture and the tension in her eyes reminded me of the Mare I used to know. She looked downtrodden, yet erect. She was dried up. A loveless life will do that to you. I hadn't met people like these before, but here they were a frequent sight. Life left a harsh mark on them as they grew old.

I knew why she'd come.

I was sitting at the table when she entered. I looked up from the notebooks I'd just finished evaluating.

"Do you think I'll let Filio fall into your absurd whirlpool of insanity? You and Kata disgust me, and it is time you know this. You disgust me with the loathsome thoughts you swear by. You're nothing but the product of sick minds. Get out of my house."

"Don't you forget that it's our house, and that we set the rules. You'll move Filio to the ground floor today, or she'll be taken away and you'll never see her again. We have an appropriate place for her, where she can be of use."

Dear God, what is she trying to tell me, I thought frightened, and knew I wouldn't let Filio become part of this life. I couldn't bear to have her taken away. Their threats are to be taken seriously. I have no one to turn to. I haven't seen the Commander nearby for years. I don't seek him out, and he no longer sees me. On Sundays, he walks with bowed head past the group of women who are still waiting for him. He's as dried up as Mare. He simply has no reason to be or to take his leave. That's about it.

I'll move Filio, of course I will, I have no other option. It's hard. Nothing has ever been harder.

*   *   *

In the morning Filio and I stood in front of the church. She had asked me to come along. For years I've gone nowhere but to the school, met other people only occasionally. We stood at the back, like I used to do with my daughter and Uri. Those were good but strange times.

She's entered the game. I sensed her confusion and thought how I'd never lowered my eyes in front of the church the way Filio did today.

She's lost the privileges I had. Is she suffering? Does she really want to be with them? Have the lustful birds of the island moved into her and changed her? Is she still mine?

She lifted her head for a brief moment when the men walked past us. Who was she looking for? Did I only imagine she was clenching her fists and teeth? Her trepidation was so powerful that I shifted my legs. I've never felt the restlessness stronger than today, standing next to Filio. It was either happiness or anxiety, I couldn't tell which. I remembered my early years here. My anticipation to see the Commander. Who are they waiting for since they don't know which one of the men lay on top of them? They can only guess, sense.

All this is madness. I left. First time ever I didn't follow them into the church.

*   *   *

Nothing has changed between the two of us. We talked in the morning. I gazed at her face. She's beautiful, with big eyes and translucent skin, but she didn't seem happy or at ease. She searched for her guilt on my face. She won't find it. It's not her fault. I knew it would hurt her. I'm proud that she didn't fall. Walking is easier.

I put my arm around her shoulders and walked her to the door. She's grown taller over the past few months, her body has become more rounded. She's become a woman.

"My man is at my place, Helena. And it's already daylight," she led me to the window. "It's day but he is sitting there, by the window, waiting for me to come home from school. He says that my sons remember me when they pass by in front of the church. He pointed me out to them, he said."

We laughed quietly, thinking of those years when we couldn't even fathom such a thought. Humans will be humans. They have a violent streak in them, like it or not.

"He'll stay until the evening. How I've waited for him! He never said it out loud, like today: 'I will come often,' he said, 'and I will be the only one. Those others who may come will just sit with you for awhile, so that nobody finds out. It's not too late? The Commander allows us to make our own arrangements. He asked me to be careful, only a few of us dare, others still obey the rules. It's still dangerous,' he told me. I really wanted him, Helena, and I got him. Do I deserve this? I guess so."

We walked to the school. All morning singing could be heard from her classroom. Will she go through all the music material today? My dear, sweet Lana.

*   *   *

I hadn't seen Filio all day. I looked for her in her room. She wasn't there. I went upstairs. She lay there, pale and quiet, covered up to her chin, and asked for food, for a lot of food. "I want to eat," she said. "Give me the best there is."

After a few days she grew even quieter. She stopped talking altogether. A strange obstinacy had moved into her body, or was it rebellion? She won't last. Something's bound to happen. All I can do is wait.

*   *   *

Filio has left. She's been gone for a few days. Only today did they notice her absence. I knew it the very first day. I found on the doorstep a bunch of flowers from the meadow above the town where we're not allowed to go. I knew it, and I waited.

Lana was always in the know about what was happening in the Lower town; this time as well. They launched a search for Filio on the open sea, but it was days after she'd disappeared, and they found nothing. I've been terrified that she might have been caught and locked up somewhere. Lana will know. I have to wait to find out. I haven't slept for days.

*　　*　　*

I'm sitting by the window, just like at the beginning. I don't stir, am interested in nothing. There's only a small detail I need to write down. Lana has made inquiries. She's certain that Filio is no longer on the island. Now I can just sit, sit.

On the morning of her flight I went into her room. Only the furniture was left. Later I handled the objects which she'd moved into her childhood room upstairs. I went to the cellar and lit the corner where I'd hidden the case with gold coins. It was gone. I was glad that she'd understood my hints about leaving.

She was found on the continent. I heard news some months ago. She's bought a house and is going to school. She lives alone and sees no one.

They'll let her stay there.

Translated by Sonja Kravanja.

Billie Holiday

Andrej Blatnik

What if, she says, we played that old Billie Holiday record? Would you kiss me then?

You don't have it any more, he says. You don't have that record any more.

How do you know? she asks. There are some things one never loses.

But not that record, he says. Do you remember how we searched for it last year? That time we went to the cinema and were both very sad afterwards, and we got drunk and looked for that record and it wasn't anywhere, and we just danced, without music. Don't you remember?

Yes, I remember, she says. But we got drunk that time and we didn't look everywhere. The record could have still been someplace, it's just that we didn't find it that time.

And you found it afterwards? he asks. You?

I do the cleaning in this apartment, in case you've already forgotten, she says quietly. I'm the one who goes rummaging through the closets.

And now you have it? Do you have it? he asks, a trifle impatiently.

It doesn't matter, she says quietly. I don't think it matters.

No? he says. You don't?

You didn't answer my question, she says. You didn't tell me.

What? he says.

Well, she says, if you'd kiss me.

If I had the record.

What does that mean—if I had?

It's mine, isn't it? You bought it for me, for my birthday. Don't you remember?

He remains silent.

Yes, I remember, he says slowly. Yes, that's right.

It's also written on it, she says. It says: to you, the one and only. And your name is on it. And the date.

Is it? he says.

Yes. Don't you remember?

I remember, he says, quite slowly, not sounding very convinced.

You've forgotten, she says, you've forgotten. To you, the one and only. You forgot everything. And you won't even kiss me any more. Not even if I play that record. Because you think it's too late. Don't you?

What? he says.

Don't be evasive, she says. You know what I'm talking about. That's what you think, isn't it?

He says nothing. When he finally breaks the silence, his voice is hoarse and breaks against the walls of the room.

Wouldn't it be better, he says, if people solved things like this in some other way? Differently?

In what way? she asks. How differently?

With less...pain. More easily.

And how do you imagine that? she says slowly.

Let's say: write about it to the papers. And then people would respond. Give advice. They would say: it happened to me too, and then...

Dear Abby?

Dear Abby.

And how would this help? Advice? We've had more than enough advice, everybody told us their story, everyone has one. And it was no use.

Even if it was no use, he says. It would be there. It's easier if you know you're not the only one it's happened to.

You mean like you said the other day, that it's necessary to distribute the pain equally? she asks. That everyone gets an equal share of it? And that this way it's easier for everyone?

Yes, he nods seriously. That's it.

Interesting, she says. Interesting.

What, he asks. What's interesting?

She opens her mouth, and he, against his will, notices how this mouth is smaller than the one he remembers. Something is missing, he thinks. No, not missing—it's grown smaller.

The telephone rings.

The phone's ringing, she says.

I can hear it, he says, it's ringing. And now what?

Answer it. Pick it up. It's for you, I'm sure.

What if it isn't? Maybe it's for you.

It's never for me, she says. Nobody ever calls me. It is for you.

He picks up the receiver. Hello? he says. Oh, it's you, he says then. How are you?

While the voice on the other end of the line is answering, he covers the receiver with his palm and whispers: You were right. It really is for me.

It's her, isn't it? she says.

It's her, he nods seriously, and then immediately says into the receiver: Oh, yeah? Is that so? Really?

She turns and leaves the room. He keeps glancing at her, while speaking smoothly into the telephone: Mhm. Yes. You don't say!

Music is heard from the adjoining room. He frowns and says into the telephone: What?

She returns, leans against the wall and looks at him. The corners of her mouth curve, and then drop again. And a few more times like that.

He says into the telephone: This? Billie Holiday.

She nods. Yes, Billie Holiday, she says quietly.

He says: Old, of course it's old.

She steps close to him and puts her arms around his waist.

He says: I like it.

She leans her head against his belly.

He says: What? No, I'm not alone.

She gives him a strong hug.

He says: She's here. Near me.

She draws his shirt out of his pants.

He says: What do you mean, how near? Yes, she's in this room. Yes, close enough to touch.

She draws her palm across his skin.

He says, somewhat reluctantly: I don't know. He covers the receiver and mouths a question. She says, loudly, as if they were alone: What?

He keeps covering the receiver, and whispers: She's asking if you mind my talking to her.

I do mind, she says calmly. And continues to caress his skin.

He removes his hand from the receiver and wipes the sweat from his forehead. She doesn't mind, he says unconvincingly into the telephone.

Did she fall for it? she asks.

He nervously covers the receiver with his hand.

What? he says. No, that's music. Billie Holiday.

She rises, steps close to him and kisses him on the mouth.

He takes hold of her chin and turns her face away, but not with much conviction.

Of course I love you, he says into the receiver.

Tell her you're lying, she says quietly. Tell her.

Really, he says. I do.

You know you love me, she says with determination. Me. Although you don't show it. Although you think you shouldn't show it.

He lets the hand holding the receiver dangle at his hip. How do you know? he says.

Your skin tells me, she says calmly. At night, when we're lying together, in the same bed, your skin tells me: I love you.

How's that? he says. My skin?

Skin talks, she says with conviction. Didn't you know?

No, I didn't, he admits.

There's a lot more you don't know, it seems to me, she says, somehow compassionately.

He looks at her for a while, then drops his eyes and notices the receiver in his hand. What did you say? he says. And waits.

Then he hangs up.

She's no longer there, he says.

That's the way it should be, she says. She hung up. She knew you were lying. Like I know.

No, he objects, I'm not lying.

The skin, she says. Your skin gives you away.

My skin? he says and draws his palm across his cheek. What's all this about skin?

Yeah, what about it? she asks. Why don't you listen to it any more? Why don't you follow it? Why do you want to get out of it?

Listen? Follow? Out? he asks. Hey, listen, what's your game? What are you trying to tell me?

That you don't know how to listen, she says calmly. And that's why you think that all things come to an end. That they pass away and are gone. That they disappear without a trace. While in reality they're still there, only different. If you listened, you'd know.

I don't understand, he says.

You don't understand because you don't listen, she says. Everything lasts. It's true that it sometimes isn't the way it used to be, it's true that it sometimes looks old and out of style. But it lasts. Just a sort of film covers it. And everything is the same as it used to be. The same beautiful things. Just a little...older. And that's why they look strange to you.

Like Billie Holiday? he says. Beautiful, but old. And that's why it crackles.

That's right. Like Billie Holiday.

But we lost it, he says to himself.

And found it again, she says.

You found it, he says. You. I... I'm just listening. From a distance.

Once you said, she says, that everything looked beautiful that way. From a distance. Because you could imagine it your way.

Once, he says, once I had all the answers. I knew everything. What. Why. How.

And now it's over, she says. You don't have any answers any more. But you still have something. Something more.

What? he asks.

Me, she says. You've got me.

I can't, he says. You know it doesn't work that way.

What way? she asks.

You're not enough. I have to eat. I have to sleep, I have to...

What? she says. What else? Tell me.

What else am I supposed to say? he says.

Her, she says. You haven't mentioned her.

Why does it always end with her? he says, bad-tempered. Why does everything lead to her in the end?

Yes, why? she says thoughtfully. Why, when in reality...

The music stops.

What is it? he starts. Is it the end of the record?

Wait, she says. There's more.

And really, in the next room Billie Holiday starts singing again.

The sky was blue
And high above
The moon was new
And so was love...

That's what you sang to me when we were at the seaside, he grows tender.

No, no, she says.

Yes, he continues. Quite a while ago. When we walked along the beach in the evening, and you told me which star was which. I was absolutely enchanted; I don't know anything about stars.

No, no, she persists.

Yes, nothing. And then we sat down somewhere by the sea. It looked like the middle of nowhere, remember? And we drank all the fruit-brandy we could get into that little flask you gave me when you were selling them at the Christmas fair. And you held my hand a little longer every time I handed you the drink.

That wasn't me, she says with determination.

No? he says incredulously.

No.

That's right, he grows pensive. Her skin was cooler than yours.

Was it?

Yes. Cool and smooth.

And mine isn't?

I know every pore of your skin.

Pore? she says.

Crease and scratch, he says, somewhat impatiently.

And that's why you don't want it any more, she says calmly. Are there many?

I don't know, he says. But I know them all.

They do no harm, she says. It's like Billie Holiday's records.

Scratches belong there. Without them it would be something different.

That's just it, he says.

It—what?

It—something different.

So that's what it's all about, she says. You're fed up. And you think it'll take your mind off it, if it's something different. And that you won't notice that it's sometimes the same as it was before. Because you're the same. It's the same, except for the scratches that come after a long time.

No, he says. What are you talking about? That's nonsense.

Nonsense, she nods. As always. The same, I tell you.

The telephone rings again.

Let it ring, she says. It'll stop.

Aren't you interested in who it is? he asks. It might be for you.

I know who it is, she says. It's not for me.

If it isn't for you, he says, then it's for me. And if it's for me, I really don't see why I shouldn't answer it.

Because you don't have time, she says.

I don't have time? What am I doing that is so important that I don't have time?

You're listening to Billie Holiday.

I think I can listen to Billie Holiday and talk on the phone. Both at the same time. I think I can manage that.

No, you can't. Not if you listen to Billie Holiday and kiss me at the same time. Then you can't talk on the phone.

Listen to Billie Holiday and kiss you? Like in the old times?

That's right. Only with more scratches. With the coating. With everything that came along. And so, differently.

But look, the phone won't stop ringing. It just keeps ringing. I can't listen to Billie Holiday with the phone ringing all the time. I can't kiss you if it's ringing, and it's for me, and I know who it is.

Well, then answer and tell her, she says. Tell her what you're doing. And it'll stop ringing. And it'll be easier.

He looks at her. He looks at the telephone. He looks at his hand hovering over the receiver.

I should tell her? Really? And if I do tell her—what'll happen then? Will it be any different? Changed in any way?

Tell her. There are things that don't seem to exist unless you say them. Maybe this one isn't that kind... But then, maybe it is. Tell her, and we'll see what happens next.

He picks up the receiver. He looks at her again, and she nods. He also lifts his head and bends it upon his chest in a slow arc. Singing is still heard from the background. The record is crackling slightly.

I can't, he says into the receiver held in his outstretched arm, far away from his mouth. I can't. I'm listening to Billie Holiday. Still. In the same way. But differently. Do you hear? Do you understand?

Translated by Tamara Soban.

Notes on the Contributors

Andrej Blatnik (b. 1963) received his M.A. in American Literature from the University of Ljubljana and attended the International Writing Program at the University of Iowa as a Fulbright fellow. He is an editor at Cankarjeva založba publishing house and has served on the editorial board of *Literatura* since 1984. He has published two novels, *Plamenice in solze* (Torches and tears, 1987) and *Tao ljubezni* (Closer to love, 1996), and three collections of short stories, most recently *Menjave kož* (1990), published by Northwestern University Press in 1998 as *Skinswaps*. He has published radio dramas, English translations, a collection of essays on contemporary American literature and a book of cultural criticism.

Berta Bojetu-Boeta (1946-1997) was educated at the Academy of Performing Arts in Ljubljana and worked as an actress. One of the very few practicing Slovenian Jews, she published two collections of poetry, *Žabon* (Male frog, 1979) and *Besede iz hise Karlstein* (Words from the house of Karlstein, 1988), and two puppet plays. She is best known for her novels *Filio ni doma* (Filio is not at home, 1990) and *Pticja hisa* (The birdhouse, 1995). Her novels have been translated into Bosnian.

Aleš Debeljak (b. 1961) graduated in comparative literature from the University of Ljubljana and received his Ph.D. in social thought from Syracuse University. He has published six collections of poetry, including *Anxious Moments* (White Pine Press, 1994), and six books of essays and cultural criticism, including *Reluctant Modernity: The Institution of Art and its Historical Forms* (Rowman and Littlefield, 1998) and *Twilight of the Idols: Recollections of a Lost Yugoslavia* (White Pine Press, 1994). A recipient of the Prešeren Foundation Prize/ National Book Award, he has held a Fulbright and fellowships from Budapest Institute of Advanced Study and from the University of California-Berkeley. He chairs the cultural studies department at the University of Ljubljana.

Milan Dekleva (b. 1946) graduated in comparative literature and literary theory from the University of Ljubljana. He has published ten collections of poetry, most recently *Šepavi soneti* (Limping sonnets, 1995), *Anaximander* (1990), *Odjedanje božjega* (Eating-away of the divine, 1988), and *Narečje telesa* (The body accent, 1987). He has also published essays, translations, three plays, and a few children's books and musicals. A composer and jazz pianist, he works as a journalist for several newspapers and for television.

Niko Grafenauer (b. 1940) graduated in comparative literature from the University of Ljubljana. He has published seven books of poetry, most recently *Samota* (Solitude, 1994), *Elegije* (Elegies, 1990), and *Palimpsesti* (Palimpsests, 1984), as well as nine children's books, five books of essays, and translations from the German and Serbo-Croatian. Formerly a freelance writer and editor at the Mladinska Knjiga publishing house, he currently edits the cultural monthly *Nova revija* and its affiliated publications. He has won the Prešeren Prize for lifetime achievement.

Maja Haderlap (b. 1961, Eisenkappel) graduated in theater studies from the University of Vienna, Austria. She has published two collections of poetry, *Zalik pesmi* (Fortune poems, 1983) and *Bajalice* (Divining rods, 1987), for which she was awarded the Prešeren Foundation Prize/ National Book Award. She translates from and into German as well as writing criticism, particularly on literature by the Slovenian minority in Austria. She works as a literary manager at the Klagenfurt Municipal Theater and is editor of the literary magazine *Mladje* in the Carinthia region of Austria, where she lives.

Andrej Inkret (b. 1934) was educated at the Academy of Performing Arts in Ljubljana, worked as a stage manager in the National Theater and later as a newspaper journalist. After receiving a Ph.D. in theater studies, he became a professor at the Academy, where he was a playwright, editor of various literary magazines, book reviewer, critic of avant-garde theater, and cultural commentator. He has published more than ten books of criticism and reviews, for which he was awarded the Prešeren Foundation Prize/ National Book Award in 1981.

Drago Jančar (b. 1948) graduated from the Law College in Maribor. A past president of the Slovenian P.E.N. Center, he is currently an editor at Slovenska matica, the oldest Slovenian intellectual association. His most recent novel, *Posmehljivo poželenje* (1993), was published in 1998 by Northwestern University Press as *Mocking Desire*. The author of more than twenty books, he has published short story collections, plays, screenplays and essays, and is the most frequently translated fiction writer in Slovenia. A former Fulbright fellow, he won the Prešeren Foundation Prize/ National Book Award in 1993 and the European Short Story Award in 1994.

Milan Jesih (b. 1950) studied comparative literature in Ljubljana. In the

1960s he was a member of an avant-garde literary-performance group before growing disillusioned with ideological and aesthetic projects. He has published more than ten books of poems, including *New Sonnets* (1995), *Soneti* (Sonnets, 1991), *Usta* (Mouth, 1985), *Volfram* (1980) and *Uran v urinu, gospodar* (Urine in urine, Lord, 1972), and his work has been translated into several European languages. He has written radio plays and translated over forty plays. He won the Prešeren Foundation Prize/ National Book Award in 1986.

Majda Kne (b. 1954) studied Slovenian language and comparative literature in the Faculty of Arts at the University of Ljubljana. She is the author of the poetry collections *Popisovanje in rondo* (Cataloguing and rondeau, 1978) and *Ko bo s čudovito gladkim gibom ukazala finale* (When with a wonderfully smooth movement she'll order finale, 1980). The winner of an all-Yugoslav Award for Young Writers, she currently writes cultural criticism for several newspapers and works as a bookseller.

Edvard Kocbek (1904-1981) studied theology and Romance languages in Germany and France and graduated in Slavic literatures from the University of Ljubljana in 1930. In 1941 he helped to found the National Liberation Front, holding various positions as a representative of the Christian Socialist Party, but was forced to withdraw from politics after his prose collection *Strah in pogum* (Fear and courage) appeared in 1951. He published ten poetry collections, including *Zemlja* (Soil, 1934), *Groza* (Horror, 1963) and *Žerjavica* (Glow, 1974), and more than twenty books of fiction, essays, memoirs and war journals. He won the Prešeren Prize for lifetime achievement in 1964. The biligual *Na vratih zvečer/At the Door at Evening* was published by Muses & Co. in Quebec in 1993.

Ciril Kosmač (1910-1980) was born on the Slovenian ethnic territory that was controlled by Italy during the world wars. After spending time in an Italian prison on nationalist charges, he emigrated to Yugoslavia. In 1938 he moved to Paris and later lived in London. In 1944 he joined the partisan resistance, and after the war he worked as a journalist and in the nascent Slovenian film industry. Best known for his novel *Pomladni dan* (A day in spring, 1953), he wrote several short story collections, and his novella *Balada o trobenti in oblaku* (The ballad of a trumpet and a cloud, 1968) served as the basis for a well-known Slovenian film.

Kajetan Kovič (b. 1931) graduated in comparative literature from the University of Ljubljana. He is a former journalist and editor-in-chief of Državna založba Slovenije. His books of poetry include *Prezgodnji dan* (Premature day, 1956), *Korenine vetra* (The roots of wind, 1961), *Ogenjvoda* (Firewater, 1965), *Mala čitanka* (A Small Reader, 1973), *Labrador* (1976), *Dežele* (Lands, 1988), *Sibirski ciklus* (The Siberian cycle, 1992) and *Lovec* (The hunter, 1993). He has also published five books for children, five novels, and a collection of short stories. A member of the Slovenian Academy of Arts and Sciences, he translates German, French, Russian, Czech and Hungarian poetry. In 1978 he won the Prešeren Prize for lifetime achievement.

Meta Kušar (b. 1952) graduated in Slovenian literature and Serbian-Croatian literatures from the University of Ljubljana. Her collections of poetry include *Maderia*, published in 1993 in both Slovenian-Italian and Slovenian-English editions, and *Svila in lan/Silk and Flax* (bilingual, 1997). She is an essayist and directed poetry reading series and other literary events at the Plečnik Bookstore in Ljubljana, where she worked until recently. She has produced and directed over sixty radio programs on cultural-art historical themes and relevant literary figures, including a full-length video portrait of a leading contemporary theater actor published earlier this year.

Svetlana Makarovič (b. 1939) graduated in stage-acting from the Academy for Theater and Film in Ljubljana. She has published more than ten collections of poetry, including *Tisti čas* (That time, 1993), *Pesmi o Sloveniji* (Poems on Slovenia, 1984), *Sosed gora* (Neighbor mountain, 1980), *Pelin žena* (Poison woman, 1974), *Srčevec* (Heart stuff, 1973), *Volčje jagode* (Wolf's berries, 1972), *Kresna noč* (Midsummer's night, 1968) and *Somrak* (Twilight, 1964). She has worked as an actress, free-lance writer, singer-songwriter, playwright, and children's book author and illustrator. She won the 1994 Jenko Award.

Miloš Mikeln (b. 1930) studied at the Academy of Performing Arts in Ljubljana and has worked as a theater director, journalist, and publishing house director. He is a former president of the Slovenian P.E.N. Center and in 1984 initiated the formation of the Writers for Peace Committee of International P.E.N., of which he served as chair for a decade. He is the author of five books of satirical prose and numerous cabaret, theater and radio plays. His biography of Stalin was translated into Serbian, Hungarian and Polish, while his epic novel *Veliki voz* (The Great Bear) won The Novel of the Year Award for 1992.

Boris A. Novak (b. 1953, Belgrade) received his Ph.D. in comparative litera-ture from the University of Ljubljana. He is a former editor of *Nova revija* and past president of the Peace Committee of International P.E.N. His col-lections of poetry include *Stihožitje* (Still-life-in-verse, 1977), *Hči spomina* (Daughter of memory, 1981), *1001 stih* (1001 verses, 1983), *Kronanje* (Coronation, 1984) and *Vrtnar tišine/ Gardener of Silence* (bilingual, 1990). He has also published plays, children's radio plays, and translations from the French and English. In 1984 he won the Prešeren Foundation Prize/ National Book Award, and in 1991 served as American Bank Visiting Professor of Humanities at the University of Tennessee-Chattanooga.

Boris Pahor (b. 1913, Trieste) received his Ph.D. from the University of Padua. His prose works include *Mesto v zalivu* (A Town in a Bay, 1955), *Zatemnitev* (Blackout, 1975), and *V labirintu* (In the labyrith, 1984). He has published numerous essays, and his memoir *Nekropola* (1967) was published by Harcourt Brace as *Pilgrim Among the Shadows* (1995) and in France as *Pelerin parmi les ombres* (1995). He lives in Trieste.

Gregor Strniša (1930-1987) held an M.A. in Germanic studies and worked as a free-lance writer. His books of poetry include *Mozaiki* (Mosaics, 1959), *Odisej* (Odyssey, 1963), *Zvezde* (Stars, 1965), *Želod* (Acorn, 1972), *Mirabilia* (1973), *Oko* (Eye, 1974), *Škarje* (Scissors, 1975) and *Vesolje* (Universe, 1983). He also wrote four verse plays, including *Žabe ali prilikia o ubogem in bogatem Lazarju* (Frogs, or exemplarium about the poor and rich Lazarus, 1969) and *Driada* (Dryads, 1976), radio plays and fiction for young adults, and his song lyrics have become part of the larger cultural consciousness. He was award-ed the Prešeren Prize for lifetime achievement in 1986.

Tomaž Šalamun (b. 1941, Zagreb) graduated in art history from the University of Ljubljana and from the International Writing Program at the University of Iowa. Since his two books in samizdat, *Poker* (1966) and *The Purpose of the Cloak* (1968), he has published more than twenty collections of poetry. His recent books in English translation are *The Four Questions of Melancholy: New and Selected Poems* (White Pine Press, 1997), *The Shepherd, The Hunter* (Pedernal, 1992) and *Selected Poems* (Ecco, 1988). He is a past Fulbright fellow at Columbia University and cultural attaché to the

Slovenian Consulate General. He was recently awarded the Prešeren Prize for lifetime achievement, and his *Book for My Brother* is forthcoming from Harcourt Brace.

Ivo Štandeker (1961-1992) studied German and comparative literature at the University of Ljubljana. He translated theoretical texts by Hegel, Freud and Habermas as well as a book of Mozart's letters into Slovenian. He also translated essays on psychoanalysis by Slovenian authors into German. In the late 80s he was affiliated with the weekly *Mladina*, for which he wrote a regular column on the art of cartoon drawing while mentoring young illustrators. After covering the Ten Day War as a journalist, he traveled through Croatia and Bosnia, reporting on the war and its consequences. He was killed by a Serbian sniper in the summer of 1992.

Veno Taufer (b. 1933) graduated in comparative literature from the University of Ljubljana. He edited the literary magazine *Revija 57* until it was banned in 1959. His fourteen books of poetry include *Svinčene zvezde* (Lead stars, 1958), *Vaje in naloge* (Exercises and assignments, 1969), *Pesmarica rabljenih besed* (A songbook of used words, 1975), *Vodenjaki* (Water People, 1986) and *Črepinje pesmi* (Shards of a poem, 1990). He founded the international literary festival Vilenica in 1986 and directed it for over a decade. He has published theater criticism, children's books, translations and a play. A past Fulbright fellow at the University of Maryland, he won the Central European Award in 1995 and the Prešeren Prize for lifetime achievement in 1996.

Jože Udovič (1912-1986) graduated in Slavic literatures from the University of Ljubljana. During the Second World War he was interned in an Italian concentration camp and in 1943 joined the partisan movement. Later he worked as a free-lance writer and translator of French, German, English, Russian and Spanish poetry and fiction. His five collections of poetry include *Ogledalo sanj* (A mirror of dreams, 1961), *Darovi* (Gifts, 1975) and *Oko in senca* (The eye and the shadow, 1982). He published a number of essays and novellas as well as a book of his journals. A member of the Slovenian Academy of Arts and Sciences, he was awarded the Prešeren Prize for lifetime achievement in 1962.

Dane Zajc (b. 1929) graduated from a secondary school in Ljubljana where he later worked as librarian. He helped to found the literary magazines *Revija 57, Problemi,* and *Perspektive,* which he edited. He is a past president of the Slovenian Writers' Association and a former Fulbright fellow at Columbia University. His books of poetry include *Požgana trava* (Burnt grass, 1958), *Jezik iz zemlje* (A tongue of soil, 1961), *Ubijavci kač* (Snake killers, 1968), *Si videl* (Did you see, 1979) and *Zarotitve* (Incantations, 1985). He has published five plays and four books of poetry for children. He received the Prešeren Prize for lifetime achievement in 1981, and his *Zbrana dela* (Collected works) was published in five volumes in 1990.

Vitomil Zupan (1914-1987) spent five years in prison during and after the Second World War. He went on to graduate in architecture and civil engineering from the University of Ljubljana and worked as a free-lance writer. The majority of his early work, including *Klement* (1974) and the much-translated *Menuet za kitaro* (Minuet for the Guitar, 1975), was not published until the 1970s. His later prose works include *Komedija cloveskega tkiva* (The Comedy of Human Flesh, 1980), *Levitan* (Leviathan, 1983) and *Človek letnih časov* (A Man of the Seasons, 1987). He also wrote poetry, drama, radio plays, screenplays, and books for teenagers.

THE EDITOR

Andrew Zawacki graduated in English and history from the College of William and Mary. As a Rhodes Scholar he earned an M.Phil. in modern English literature and society from Oxford University and an M.Litt. in creative writing from the University of St. Andrews. He is co-editor of the international journal *Verse*. His poetry and criticism have appeared in *The New Republic, Times Literary Supplement, Boston Review* and elsewhere in the U.S., U.K., Ireland and Australia. A former fellow of the Slovenian Writers' Association, he has been a contributor to *Književni Listi, Nova revija, Literatura* and *Večer,* and has participated in both the Vilenica and the Dnevi Poezije in Vina festivals. He has held fellowships from the Salzburg Seminar in American Studies and Hawthornden Castle International Retreat. He is currently a doctoral candidate in the Committee on Social Thought at the University of Chicago.

This is an extension of the copyright page.

The Case of Slovenia, several editors (Ljubljana: Nova revija, 1991); *Edvard Kocbek: Poems*, edited by Aleš Debeljak (*Litterae Slovenicae* 2, XXXIII, 86; Ljubljana: Slovenian Writers' Association, 1995); *Dane Zajc: A Monograph*, edited by Tatjana Pregel Kobe (Ljubljana: Edina Press, 1997); *Kajetan Kovič Poems* (*Litterae Slovenicae* 2, XXV, 91; Ljubljana: Slovenian Writers' Association, 1997); Poetry Miscellany Chapbook Series, edited by Richard Jackson (Chattanooga, TN: 1991-1995); *Prisoners of Freedom: Contemporary Slovenian Poetry*, edited by Aleš Debeljak (Santa Fe, NM: Pedernal, 1994); *The Four Questions of Melancholy: New and Selected Poems* by Tomaž Šalamun, edited by Christopher Merrill (Fredonia, NY: White Pine Press, 1997); *Svila in lan/ Silk and Flax* by Meta Kušar, edited by Matej Bogataj (Ljubljana: DZS, 1997); *The Veiled Landscape: Slovenian Women Writing*, edited by Zdravko Duša (Ljubljana: Slovenian Office for Women's Policy, 1995); *Anxious Moments* by Aleš Debeljak (Fredonia, NY: White Pine Press, 1994); *Double Vision: Four Slovenian Poets*, edited by Richard Jackson (Chattanooga, TN & Ljubljana: Poetry Miscellany Books & Aleph Press, 1993); *A Day in Spring* by Ciril Kosmač (Ljubljana: Slovenian Writers' Association, 1988); *Minuet for the Guitar* by Vitomil Zupan (Ljubljana: Slovenian Writers' Association, 1988); *Veliki voz* by Miloš Mikeln (Ljubljana: Knjižna zadruga, 1992); *Filio is Not at Home* by Berta Bojetu-Boeta (Ljubljana & Klagenfurt: Wieser, 1990); *The Day Tito Died: Contemporary Slovenian Short Stories* (London & Boston, MA: Forest Books, 1993); *Vilenica Desetnica, 1986-1995*, edited by Veno Taufer (*Litterae Slovenicae* 1, XXXIII, 85; Ljubljana: Slovenian Writers' Association, 1995); several volumes of *Vilenica Almanac*, edited by Veno Taufer; *Le Livre Slovène*; *Verse*.

While every effort has been made to locate the copyright holders of texts and translations, comments and corrections are appreciated for all future editions.

I would like to thank the Slovenian Writers' Association for a generous fellowship that enabled me to begin editing this anthology—particularly Barbara Stanič for her efficient help with numerous quandaries both on-line and off; Barbara Šubert for travel tips and daily hints about the local lay of the land; Veno and Jasna Taufer for showing me Pleterje monastery and other Slovenian solitudes; Gregor Kiseljak for a cup a day of barcaffé; and Lidija Vakselj for insuring I didn't go broke. Thank you to the many Slovenian writers and critics who gave not only their time and talents to this project but also their trust to how it might turn out. Thanks to the organizers of Vilenica for their hospitality, to Aleš Šteger for days of poetry and to Alex Klinec for wine to go with, and to the Rhodes Scholarship Trust for travel grants that allowed me to attend both festivals. Many thanks to the editors of *Književni Listi, Literatura, Nova revija* and *Večer*, for allowing me to discuss American-Slovenian poetic relations in their pages, and to the Beletrina press for an informative trip to the Belgrade Book Fair. Thank you to Tomaž Šalamun and Metka Krašovec for a clean, well-lighted place in New York and for their friendship now synonymous with that city. Many thanks to Erica Johnson Debeljak for helping me feel at home in her adopted country, and especially in her company, when everywhere else seemed foreign. Thank you to Brett Lauer of the Poetry Society of America for typing a number of the prose selections on short notice with no pay, and to my parents John and Cathryn for continually taking care of prosy items on shorter notice while paying. Thanks to Lukas Haynes for a trip to Sarajevo during the elections, for an ongoing dialogue about Balkan politics and poetics, and for his unyielding support. Thanks, as always, to my literary co-conspirator Brian Henry, who is never not there when I call, or as poetry itself requires. I am grateful to the Constance Saltonstall Foundation for the Arts for a residency to complete this book, as well as to Elaine LaMattina of White Pine Press for her editorial expertise and patience while I kept not quite getting done. My deepest thanks go to Aleš Debeljak for giving me the opportunity to edit the present volume and for serving as tireless informant and adviser along the way. His agility in crossing borders is equalled only by his admirable insistence that others cross them too. By introducing me to his country he has also taught me a great deal about my own, and now I'm no longer sure which one is whose—thank you, Mr. Vertigo, for that much and much more.

—AZ